my lie

my lie

A True Story of False Memory

Meredith Maran

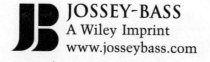
JOSSEY-BASS
A Wiley Imprint
www.josseybass.com

Published by Jossey-Bass
A Wiley Imprint
989 Market Street, San Francisco, CA 94103-1741—www.josseybass.com

Jossey-Bass books and products are available through most bookstores. To contact Jossey-Bass directly call our Customer Care Department within the U.S. at 800-956-7739, outside the U.S. at 317-572-3986, or fax 317-572-4002.

Jossey-Bass also publishes its books in a variety of electronic formats. Some content that appears in print may not be available in electronic books.

Library of Congress Cataloging-in-Publication Data

Maran, Meredith.
    My lie : a true story of false memory / Meredith Maran. – 1st ed.
        p. cm.
    Includes bibliographical references and index.
    ISBN 978-0-470-50214-3 (hardback)
    1. Maran, Meredith–Mental health.   2. False memory syndrome–Patients–California–Biography.   3. False memory syndrome–Patients–Family relationships–California.   4. Recovered memory.   5. Fathers and daughters.   I. Title.
    RC455.2.F35M34 2010
    362.196'8583690092–dc22
    [B]
                                                                    2010013843

Printed in the United States of America
FIRST EDITION
HB Printing 10 9 8 7 6 5 4 3 2 1

Make the lie big, make it simple, keep saying it,
and eventually they will believe it.

—*Adolph Hitler*

Marge, it takes two to lie. One to lie and one
to listen.

—*Homer Simpson*

For my family, with love and gratitude.
Finally.

contents

═══════════════

part three 1994–2009

author's note

This book is a work of nonfiction: my version of the truth. I've attempted to verify the statistics I cite, but for reasons that should be obvious, I regard all "facts" with skepticism, and recommend that you do the same.

Dialogue has been reconstructed based on my memories and notes. Names and details have been altered to protect the privacy of those who populate these pages. Some might have different memories or interpretations of this story. Their versions, of course, could also be true.

===

The Same Thing Happened to Me

December 2007

At 7 A.M. the Oakland hills were shrouded in fog, the steep trail carpeted with silvery eucalyptus leaves, damp and fragrant beneath my feet. My hiking buddy Joanne and I plodded silently past glistening ferns, granite outcroppings, waterfalls swollen with winter rain. As we neared Redwood Peak, we stumbled into a conversation well suited to the cover of the misty morning, the meditative mood.

"Have you ever done anything really awful?" Joanne asked me. "Something you'll always regret?"

At fifty-six I'd accrued an age-appropriate assortment of woulda-shoulda-couldas. But only one rose to the level of aching remorse.

"When I was in my thirties," I answered, "I accused my father of molesting me. I didn't see him or talk to him for eight years. I didn't let my kids see him for eight years, either. And then I realized that it wasn't true."

Joanne stared at me, her face a mask of disbelief. She said, "The same thing happened to me."

Standing sentry around us, ancient redwoods shuddered and dripped.

"Let me guess," I said. "It was the late eighties, early nineties. Someone gave you a copy of *The Courage to Heal.*

"You started having strange dreams, crying jags, trouble with sex," I went on. "You were seeing a therapist two or three times a week. Finally you remembered that your father had molested you."

"How did you know that?" Joanne asked. "I haven't talked about it for fifteen years."

The Courage to Heal sold almost two million copies," I said. "It must have happened to a whole lot of us."

"My dad died before I could apologize," Joanne said. She inhaled a ragged breath. "Is your dad still alive?"

I nodded. In the past few years my eighty-year-old father had been diagnosed with atherosclerosis, diabetes, depression, and Alzheimer's disease. With the possible exception of the diabetes, I blamed myself for all of it. Of course his heart was damaged. Of course he was depressed and wanted to forget. His daughter had been a difficult child and a raging teenager who'd grown into a family-wrecking adult.

"Are you and your dad speaking?" Joanne asked.

I nodded again. "We get along better now than we did . . . before."

Before, alternating currents of attachment and anger had arced and hissed between us. But now my dad was too addled by Alzheimer's and too wise to go on judging me. I was too mortified by the wrong I'd done, too aware of the ticking clock of the time we had left, too humbled by my own foibles as a parent to go on judging him.

"He forgave you?"

I considered Joanne's question. Above our heads, birds chirped and called, trilling a cheery cacophony. "It seems that way," I answered.

My father had spent a decade brushing off my attempts to apologize, just as he'd brushed off so many things that mattered to me long before we were estranged. His emotional detachment was the provenance of my lifelong longing; the trait that had made my accusation credible to me, to my lover, my brother, my friends and therapists. Now, that same detachment had made it easy for him to forgive me. Or appear to have forgiven me.

Since he and I had reconciled, no one else in my family had mentioned my accusation, either. Had the rift I'd caused—the not-so-grand canyon I'd carved between those who believed me and those who didn't—really healed? Or had the memory of my false memory become one of those scarred-over but still-festering family wounds?

"My brother and sisters have never forgiven me," Joanne said, her eyes deer-in-the-headlights on mine. "I don't know how I'll ever forgive myself."

As Joanne's eyes welled with tears, I asked myself the same question. And suddenly, pretending it hadn't happened wasn't an option anymore.

One in Three

We are currently living in dangerous times, similar
to Nazi Germany. Sexual abuse hysteria is
omnipresent.
> —*Richard Gardner, professor of psychiatry,*
> *Columbia University,* True and False
> Accusations of Child Sex Abuse, *1992*

In the late 1970s, a handful of feminist scholars did some ground-
breaking research and delivered some distressing news. One in
three American women and one in ten American men, they
reported, had been victims of childhood sexual abuse.

Their studies proved that incest wasn't the rare anomaly it
had long been believed to be. Incest happened often. It happened
in normal families—in the house down the street, in the bedroom
down the hall.

A psychological phenomenon called *repressed memory* had
allowed this outrage to go unacknowledged, even unknown.
As Freud had first asserted a century earlier, the impact of child
sexual abuse on young psyches was so profound that victims often
lost their memories for years or decades. Hundreds of thousands
of Americans were walking around with the time bomb of
untreated childhood sexual abuse ticking inside of them.

For better and for worse, these findings transformed incest
from a dirty little secret of American family life into an American

obsession. During the 1980s and early 1990s, several cultural icons, including Susanne Somers, former Miss America Marilyn Van Derbur, Roseanne Barr, and Oprah Winfrey went public as incest survivors. Incest memoirs hit best-seller lists. *The Color Purple*, whose protagonist had borne two of her father's babies, won the Pulitzer Prize. Sympathetic and sensational incest stories proliferated on TV news shows and after-school specials and in newspapers and magazines.

Between 1983 and 1995, hundreds of parents and day-care workers were tried for sexually abusing and ritually torturing the children in their care. Children were removed from their parents' homes. Preschools were shut down. Hundreds of perpetrators and innocents went to jail.

Reported cases of child abuse and neglect surged from 669,000 in 1976 to 2.9 million in 1993. During those years, according to *Victims of Memory* author Mark Pendergrast, up to one million families were torn apart by false accusations of sexual abuse.

Mine was one of them.

Many of these accusations were made by adult daughters who claimed to have repressed and then recovered memories of childhood molestation by their fathers.

I was one of them.

In courtrooms around the country, daughters sat sobbing on witness stands, pointing across the room at their fathers, listing the atrocities their fathers had committed against their bodies and their souls.

If I'd been just a bit more suggestible (more impulsive, more vindictive), I might have been one of them.

Here's how I became convinced that this lie was true.

In 1982, I edited a book by one of those pioneering feminist researchers. I was shocked and moved by what I learned, working on a book I'll call *The Incest Secret*. With missionary zeal— and without considering the tunnel vision, good guy–bad guy polarization, and dangerous excesses that often accompany that sort of heart-thumping fervor—I spent the next few years writing exposés of child sexual abuse for local and national newspapers and magazines.

As a journalist doing what journalists do, slouching toward objectivity, stumbling over my preexisting prejudices and proclivities, I helped to spread the panic: basing conclusions on skewed studies I believed to be accurate, citing manipulated statistics I trusted, quoting experts who proved more loyal to their points of view than they were to the facts.

Along with other writers on both sides of the issue, I avoided using quotation marks to declare my allegiance, calling it recovered memory, not "recovered memory"; incest survivor, not "incest survivor"; "false memory syndrome," not False Memory Syndrome.

I didn't just hand out the Kool-Aid. I drank it. I didn't just write about recovered memories; I spent a decade trying to recover my own. Shortly after the 1988 publication of the Bible of the recovered-memory movement, *The Courage to Heal*, I joined the ranks of self-identified incest survivors and accused my father of molesting me.

Early in the 1990s, the backlash began.

In March 1992, accused parents banded together to form the False Memory Syndrome Foundation (FMSF). "When the memory is distorted, or confabulated," the FMSF newsletter opined, "the result can be what has been called the False Memory Syndrome; a condition in which a person's identity and interpersonal relationships are centered around a memory of traumatic experience which is objectively false but in which the person strongly believes."

Although false memory syndrome was the invention of laypeople, the phrase took on the luster of a medical diagnosis and burned its way across the country, setting off the firestorm that would come to be known as "the memory war." Even characterizing the conflict was cause for controversy. Was the "outing" of child sexual abuse a brave crusade to save children's lives, or a witch hunt reminiscent of others in the American hall of shame?

Nearly overnight, "false memory" replaced "recovered memory" on the American tongue. Therapists were sued for implanting false memories, stripped of their licenses, and ordered to pay six-figure settlements to clients who'd once credited them with saving their incest-ravaged lives. Accused molesters' convictions were overturned. Many but not all of the accused were set free.

Families already devastated by incest accusations were bifurcated by warring beliefs about truth and memory. If the outraged parents—*my outraged parents*—were right, they were the victims, their daughters the perpetrators. If the daughters were right, they—*we*—were the victims, our parents the perpetrators, denying the trauma they'd inflicted upon us. Each side enlisted a phalanx of opposing experts who built constituencies and careers on unproved certainties.

When the culture tilted toward disbelief, I leaned that way too. In 1996, I faced the truth that my accusation was false. I apologized to my father and my family, quit incest therapy, and broke up with—truth be told, was dumped by—my incest survivor lover.

A few years later, just when I'd fully regained my mind and my memories, my father was diagnosed with Alzheimer's disease and began to lose his.

Redemption-wise, my father's diagnosis left me two options.

I could hope he'd forget the wrong I'd done him, along with the other bits and bytes that were slipping through the fissures in his brain. Or I could convince him to have a conversation with me about what I'd done and why I'd done it and how sorry I was.

A girl can dream: maybe he'd even forgive me, so I might step into that shaft of light and begin to forgive myself. But first

I needed to understand. How had I—more neurotic than some, but surely less neurotic than many—come to believe that my father, a man lacking the cruelty to squash a spider, had sexually abused me throughout my childhood and spent the next twenty years covering it up?

How had so many other people come to believe the same thing at the same time?

In *Creating Hysteria*, Joan Acocella's 1999 exposé of the sex-abuse panic of the 1980s, she wrote, "One of the most disgraceful episodes in the history of psychotherapy seems to be coming to an end."

Acocella's prediction was true, and false. The sex-abuse panic did recede. But it still hasn't come to an end.

"When you once believed something that now strikes you as absurd, even unhinged, it can be almost impossible to summon that feeling of credulity again," Margaret Talbot wrote in *The New York Times Magazine* on January 7, 2001. "Maybe that is why it is easier for most of us to forget, rather than to try and explain, the Satanic-abuse scare that gripped this country in the early 80s—the myth that Devil-worshipers had set up shop in our day-care centers, where their clever adepts were raping and sodomizing children, practicing ritual sacrifice, shedding their clothes, drinking blood and eating feces, all unnoticed by parents, neighbors and the authorities.

"Of course, if you were one of the dozens of people prosecuted in these cases, one of those who spent years in jails and prisons on wildly implausible charges, one of those separated from your own children, forgetting would not be an option. You would spend the rest of your life wondering what hit you, what cleaved your life into the before and the after, the daylight and the nightmare."

As Talbot says, the panic hasn't ended for the preschool teachers and fathers and uncles who were convicted of child sexual abuse twenty years ago and remain incarcerated today.

It hasn't ended for the children, now adults, who testified against those prisoners at age four or ten or thirty, some of whom have since acknowledged that their accusations were false.

I'm guessing it hasn't ended for the 1.8 million people who have bought copies of *The Courage to Heal*. Or for the book's coauthor, Laura Davis, whose books and workshops are focused, now, on forgiveness and reconciliation.

It hasn't ended for the tens of thousands of families still struggling to recover from false accusations made decades ago.

Most important, it hasn't ended for a society that decries the mass hysteria of Salem and McCarthyism while continuing to elect presidents, wage wars, and deny its citizens health care and civil rights based on confabulations presented as facts.

Recent American history is rife with examples of the damage done when millions of people become convinced of the same lie at the same time. Choose your favorite fiction from this list, or add your own.

The George W. Bush "victory" in the 2000 election. The list of books that Sarah Palin allegedly banned from the Wasilla Public Library. The persistent rumor that Palin's youngest son was actually her daughter's child. The allegations of Barack Obama's foreign birth, terrorist associations, reverse racism, and socialist tendencies—first promulgated to prevent his presidency, later used to attempt to derail it.

How many and how much have we lost in the seemingly endless War on Terror, triggered by the fictional connection between Saddam Hussein and the 9/11 attacks? The phrase "Weapons of Mass Destruction," invented as a cry for war, has become shorthand for cynical political manipulation and the mass, willful suspension of disbelief.

President Obama's efforts to provide Americans with health care were nearly defeated by the myth that if the program were enacted, "death panels" run by government bureaucrats would decide whether Granny lives or dies.

Gay people's right to marry (*my* right to marry) is still being denied in most of the "united" states, ostensibly to protect the heterosexual nuclear family from destruction, and—wait, it gets better—to keep American children from being recruited to homosexuality in their grade-school classrooms.

In November 2008, the *The Wall Street Journal* predicted, "In 300 years' time, our descendants—who will, of course, pride themselves on their superior rationality—will read of the recovered-memory-driven prosecutions of parents (usually fathers) as we now read of the Salem witch trials.

". . . We may expect further such episodes of popular delusion and the madness of crowds," the article warned, "unless we straighten out our thoughts about the way our minds work—or, if that is not possible, at least about how they don't work."

Hence this inquiry: an intimate look back, twenty years later, at one episode of popular delusion—mine, ours. This painful, public exposé of the way my mind worked and the way it didn't is offered up with remorse, yes, but also with a pulse of hope that I, and we, will learn from this history so we're not destined to repeat it.

Meredith Maran
Oakland, California
June 2010

part one

1576–1982

It isn't so astonishing, the number of things I can remember, as the number of things I can remember that aren't so.

—*Mark Twain (true name: Samuel Clemens)*

one

Desperate Housewife

Oedipal tendencies are not abandoned during the
infantile Oedipal period; they are abandoned at
puberty and then only if the mechanism of
displacement works successfully. . . . Removal is
the process by which interest is removed from
incestuous objects and attached to outside objects.
     —*Sidney Tarachow*, International Journal
               of Psychoanalysis, *Vol. 32, 1951*

1951–1962

When I was a little girl, my dad was my best friend, and I was his.
   During the workweek my father was the Invisible Man. But
on weekends he was my companion and coconspirator, sneaking
me milk shakes behind my mother's back, rolling his eyes at me
over her head when she protested that milk shakes didn't satisfy
her eight-ounces-of-milk-per-day rule. On Saturday mornings
he'd shake me awake at dawn and we'd slink out, leaving my
sleeping mother and baby brother behind. We'd drive to Queens
for White Castle burgers, to Canal Street for kippered salmon and
bagels, to horse farms in New Jersey to watch the yearlings train.
   My dad and I did everything together. Things he liked to do,
like hitting pop-up flies in the park. Things I liked to do, like
watching *Dick Van Dyke* and *Alfred Hitchcock Presents*, sprawled

on our scratchy wool couch. And things my mother refused to do with him, like spending Saturdays handicapping the horses at Aqueduct.

I played my dad's trumpet in my elementary school orchestra. He and I acted out the screenplays he'd written before I was born, before he had to get a job, before he had to "grow up and support a family," as he often said. We recorded his plays on the Sony reel-to-reel tape recorder we'd driven downtown together, just the two of us, to buy. My dad always let me play the lead.

My 1950s homemaker mother was the bad cop, the keeper of the child-rearing checklist, the one who made me memorize my times tables and drink my milk and brush my teeth. Her frustration and her disappointment bubbled just below the glassine surface of our smoothly functioning lives. She was too smart, too ambitious, too capable to be stuck in our Upper East Side apartment, raising her kids, nursing her resentments.

My dad was a latter-day Mad Man, a reluctant account exec who bounced from one New York advertising agency to the next. He had his frustrations, too. He stored them in the bottom drawer of his dresser: the screenplays that would never see life beyond our daddy-and-daughter productions, each with a rejection letter paper-clipped to its cover page.

Even my father's second-choice career looked better to me than my mother's. He left our apartment in a cloud of Old Spice at 8 A.M. each morning, gleaming black Florsheims freshly polished, black leather attaché case in hand, prepped and propped for his important job.

My father and I had everything in common, including this: we liked each other more than either of us liked my mother. She didn't understand us. We only understood each other. My mother was an annoying interloper, a cumulous cloud that shadowed us, threatening to rain on our parade. I found ways to put distance between her fate and mine. I found ways to nestle up to my dad.

1963–1965

When I turned twelve I sprouted breasts and bled into my Carter's underpants and lost interest in my father's plays and my father's trumpet and my father's Saturdays at the track. Everything I wanted, suddenly, was forbidden. Everything I did was wrong.

I wanted to go to the High School of Music and Art with the cool, beatnik kids. My parents sent me to the more academic, more prestigious, dorkier-than-thou Bronx High School of Science instead. *Science? Me?* Their edict ultimately served me well, but not exactly in the way they'd hoped.

1966–1971

I met a boy in my sophomore year, a boy who stood on the corner outside Bronx Science before, during, and after classes, passing out antiwar leaflets, smoking skinny, stinky joints. A boy who won the Bob Dylan look-alike contest without even trying. A boy who entered the school building only to distribute the underground newspaper he wrote and published on his very own home mimeograph machine.

The first time Carl came to my house to pick me up, my father took in his wild Jewfro, peace-sign-strewn Army surplus jacket, and holey jeans, and snapped, "Where are you taking my daughter?"

"Wherever she wants to go," Carl drawled in that sexy, I'm-above-it-all way of his.

"You are never to see that boy again," my father thundered later that night when I walked in, two hours past curfew.

"His name is Carl," I shouted. "And I love him."

"He's not good enough for you!"

"I'm fifteen years old! You can't tell me what to do."

"I just did. And your mother will be keeping tabs on you when I'm not home."

Of course I sneaked out to see Carl, and of course my mother told my father, and of course my father layered punishments onto me like bricks mortared into a retaining wall—no TV, no phone, no going out on weekends, no fun.

And just like that, my hero became my enemy. I wasn't my father's best friend anymore; I was his snarling, seething prisoner. We didn't lie around on the couch anymore, watching Hitchcock. We didn't roll our eyes at each other behind my mother's back. We screamed at each other and threatened each other and stomped off to opposite ends of our white-carpeted apartment. No matter how desperately I writhed, he wouldn't release me from the trap he'd laid. I chewed at my paws, desperate to escape.

I had a choice to make: my father's love, or Carl's.

Don't think twice, Babe, it's all right.

Amazingly, I made it to the graduation ceremony of the Bronx Science class of 1968. Not so amazingly, I was expelled before the ceremony was through.

Unbeknownst to any adult (over thirty, not to be trusted), I'd predistributed to each of my fellow grads a black armband emblazoned with a white peace sign. As preagreed, when New York's popular Mayor Lindsay appeared on the stage of the Loew's Grand Concourse Theater, three hundred preordained Leaders of Tomorrow silently raised clenched fists, peace armbands on proud display. Without hesitation, the principal strode down the aisle and yanked me out of my seat. "You! Out!" he barked.

For perhaps the first time ever, I obeyed a school administrator's orders. My parents seemed unimpressed by my newfound compliance. They dragged me to the family car, tossed me into the backseat, and advised me not to speak until spoken to. The ride home to Manhattan was not a companionable one.

Shortly thereafter, I packed a duffel bag, snuck out of my parents' Upper East Side apartment, and took the subway to Astor Place. I wasn't the only wild-haired, wild-eyed runaway schlepping her stuff down St. Mark's Place on that hot, muggy, summer-of-love day in 1968, but I'm sure I was luckier than most: welcomed with open arms and spare key at the Lower East Side brownstone where my boyfriend lived with his cool, commie parents. "Honeys, I'm home," I said, and handed a delighted Carl my duffel bag and followed him to his room.

I was glad to be free of my parents, but I missed Doug, my twelve-year-old brother, achingly. Once a week at the designated time, he'd wait in the phone booth on the corner of 83rd and Lex, and I'd call him from the $95-a-month Greenwich Village studio apartment I'd moved into with Carl.

In early 1969, my father got a job in London and moved my mother and brother there. Doug and I couldn't talk anymore; we could only write to each other, paper-thin blue aerograms stippled by our frantic ballpoint pens. Four years later, when Doug turned sixteen, he came to live in Berkeley with my new boyfriend, Sean, and me.

Left at last to their own devices, after twenty years of marriage my parents divorced.

1972–1981

For the next few years, my brother and I did pretty much the same things at pretty much the same time.

In 1974, I married Robert, a nice, normal Gentile guy, and Doug married Susie, a nice, normal Gentile gal. The four of us moved to the East Bay town of Hayward, California, and started having kids. Doug and Susie's were born in May 1978 and December 1980; Robert's and mine, in December 1978 and May 1980. We sent the cousins to the same babysitters. Our parents sent them birthday cards from two different addresses.

Flooded with hormones the day after Matthew was born, I was flooded, too, with a sudden craving for my dad. I called him from my hospital bed, hoping he'd be as excited about my baby as I was, as excited as I'd always wanted him to be about me.

"You have a grandson," I said. "His name is Matthew."

My father was silent. All I heard was his breath, labored and thick. *He's crying*, I thought. *Finally we're feeling the same thing.*

"He's so beautiful," I said. "I wish you were here."

Another silence.

"Dad?"

"Yes?" my father said in that distracted, How-soon-can-I-get-off-the-phone voice of his.

"Did you even hear a word I said?"

"Of course." I knew my father was scrambling to remember what it was. "Say hello to little Michael for me," he said finally.

"His name is *Matthew*," I said, choking back bitter tears.

In 1977, our father wrote to tell Doug and me that he was getting married. "I hope you'll meet Natalie and her two sons sometime."

In 1979, he wrote to tell us that he and Natalie were getting a divorce.

Doug and Robert and I got jobs on the last of the Bay Area auto assembly lines, GM for Doug and Robert, Ford for me. We spent fifty-eight mandatory OT hours a week "organizing the working class," building competing trucks, attempting to convince our disappointingly unenthused fellow proletarians to overthrow the bourgeoisie.

In 1980, our father married Gloria, another woman we'd never met, a woman six years older than me. My father got a job in Puerto Rico, and he and Gloria moved to a beachfront condo there.

For the next decade, my brother and I saw our father once or twice a year. He'd blow into town, take Doug and me out to dinner, recite his objections to our choices of career, politics, and spouse, buy each of us a Sony TV or a refrigerator, and disappear again.

Once, my brother and I insisted that our father invite my sister-in-law and my husband to join us for dinner. As we chewed our steaks and stirred bacon bits into our baked potatoes, our father ignored them, addressing his remarks only to Doug and me.

"You were so rude," I fumed as my father and I waited curbside for Robert to fetch the car.

My father craned his neck, scanning the parking lot, radiating annoyance. "I have no idea what you're talking about."

"I'm talking about the way you treat the people your children married. The parents of your grandchildren. Do you even know their *names*?"

"Maybe you should think about why you're so desperate for my approval," my father said without looking at me. "Maybe you married the wrong man."

When Robert pulled up, my father slid into the passenger seat and sat silently, staring straight ahead. None of us said a word during the half-hour drive to his hotel.

The word "Dad" evaporated from my vocabulary. On the rare occasions when Doug and I talked about our father, we called him by his first name. He was our kids' only grandfather, but he was a stranger to them. Increasingly he was a stranger to me.

1982

Growing up in action-packed, center-of-the-universe Manhattan prepared me poorly for where and how I found myself living at age thirty-two: with my legally wed husband and 2.0 children in a suburban San Jose ranch house at 1234 Champagne Lane, an address I couldn't have made up if I tried.

Talk about your desperate housewife. My present was such an unlikely outcome of my past that I awoke most days feeling I'd fallen down someone else's rabbit hole. Robert was a good man, loyal and funny and fiercely devoted to his kids. But since we'd met on a United Farm Workers' picket line ten years before, my life, and our marriage, had been cruising down the bored-to-death highway without any brakes.

Mondays through Fridays I climbed into my pantyhose and my Volvo, deposited the kids at the local preschool, then crawled through Silicon Valley traffic to the gray-flannel cubicle where I traded my labor power for my kids' preschool fees. If you'd told me fifteen years earlier that I'd end up as a technical writer at National Semiconductor, building chips for Reagan's Trident missiles, I would have said you'd had too much of what Alice was smoking. I'd applied to National as an assembly line worker, hoping to organize a union among the mostly immigrant female workers. Being a warm-blooded, seemingly educated person of the Caucasian persuasion, over my protests that yes, I really *did* want to work on the line, I'd been hired as a technical writer instead.

I was a stranger in a strange land, airlifted into marital and occupational monotony on the wings of some idealistic notions, emotional and political, that didn't quite fly. If I got the marriage license, I'd told myself, love would last forever. If I brought my sixties ideals to the suburbs, I'd help bring injustice to an end.

Things weren't exactly working out that way.

Desperately seeking *something*, while my sons pitched Cheerios at each other one Sunday morning, I combed the help-wanted ads for a job that might make better use of me. Listings abounded for clean room supervisors and electrical engineers, but there was a distinct dearth of opportunities for a lapsed do-gooder in search of a more meaningful life.

I pulled out my pre–Silicon Valley Rolodex and start calling old friends. Bingo. One of them knew someone who knew someone who knew that a hero of mine, whom I'll call Dr. Roselyn Taylor, was looking for a freelance editor. Taylor had founded several feminist organizations and had authored an armful of feminist books. Her antimisogynist antics had earned her a special place in my own Hall of Feminist Fame.

I called Roselyn, attempting to conceal my guru worship. We made a date to meet.

two

===

In Feminism We Trust

Discounting the experiences of incest victims has a
long history. . . . The Freudian legacy is to
discount the reality of incestuous abuse and, where
discounting is impossible, to blame the child for
being the one who wanted the sexual contact in
the first place.

—*Diana Russell*, The Secret Trauma:
Incest in the Lives of Girls
and Women, 1986

Driving from San Jose to Berkeley to meet Dr. Roselyn
Taylor, I was nervous and trying not to be. I didn't expect
much from that meeting—only that it would change my so-
called life.

Roselyn's house was easy to find. The car in her driveway
was a bumper-stickered homage to contemporary feminism.
*Women Unite to Take Back the Night. Well-Behaved Women Seldom
Make History. Porn Tells Lies About Women. I'd Rather Be
Destroying Pornography. Pornography Violates My Civil Rights.*

Short but svelte at forty-something, Roselyn was prettier
than she looked on TV. She led me to a scarred oak kitchen
table in the house she shared with a couple of other *wimmin*,
filled hand-thrown ceramic mugs with chamomile tea, and told
me about the book she was working on: *The Incest Secret.*

For the past ten years, she said, her research team had been going door-to-door in San Francisco, asking questions that hadn't been asked before.

"Were you ever molested as a child?"

"How?"

"By whom?"

"Did you tell anyone?"

Their findings would be the message in the bottle of her book.

"More than one-third of American women were sexually abused as children," Roselyn told me.

I gulped, thinking of my beautiful five-year-old niece.

"Thirty-eight percent, to be precise," Roselyn said. "But the most commonly cited study still claims that incest only happens in one percent of the population."

She rattled off a string of statistics. Adults who were molested as children are ten times more likely to sexually, physically, and emotionally abuse their own kids. Women who were sexually abused as girls suffer disproportionately high rates of mental illness, addiction, and marriage to child-abusing men. Male survivors of sexual abuse are greatly overrepresented in the prison population.

"None of it will stop until the truth is known," Roselyn said. "That's why I'm writing this book."

My pulse raced. I'd felt this sense of urgency before. When I watched the TV news reports of four little girls killed in the anti-civil-rights bombing of a Birmingham church. When I saw the photo of a naked Vietnamese girl running from her napalmed village. When I read the news reports from Jonestown, dozens of children's corpses wrapped in their parents' arms, stacked like cordwood in the Guyana jungle, purple Kool-Aid staining their lips. *I need to do something about this.*

"Are you interested?" Roselyn asked, regarding me appraisingly, running long fingers through her thatch of thick, close-cropped hair.

I envisioned the new life that was opening up in front of me, if only she'd invite me into hers. "Very," I said.

"It won't be pleasant," Roselyn said. "My statistics are disturbing. The facts are hard to face."

"I can handle it," I said.

She gave me a stack of books to read. My heart jumped: the job was mine.

Time Magazine
January 31, 1983
"Law: Out of the Mouths of Babes"

... Until lately the testimony of little children was rarely allowed in court, but that is changing ...

... How accurate is the testimony of children? Their visual powers and memories are every bit as good, or bad, as adults', contends Shirley Robinson, executive director of the Child Sexual Abuse Treatment and Training Center of Illinois. "Preschoolers can't remember their addresses," she notes, "but they can remember the print of the wallpaper in the room where they were molested."

—Laura Meyers, Magda Krance, and Burnett H. Beach

When I got home, Robert didn't just tell me he was happy for me. He showed me. He reminded me that I'd been supporting our family while he learned a trade, told me to quit my detested Silicon Valley job, and shooed me into the guest room with Roselyn's books.

Digging in, I saw that the social history of child sexual abuse could be properly divided into two eras: before Freud and after.

Circa 800 B.C., long before Freud came up with his Oedipus complex, the original Oedipus killed his father, married his mother, and thereby became king. Eventually his karma caught up with him. Oedipus died in exile, leaving the incest myth behind.

Even that innocent cherub, Cupid, is believed by many mythologists to be the product of incest between Jupiter and

Venus. Hallmark, cover your ears: Cupid has also been accused of being his own mother's lover.

Fast-forward to the year 1215 when, in an attempt to preserve the purity of the aristocratic lineage, a council convened by the aptly named Pope Innocent III forbade marriage between family members related by four degrees or less, thereby outlawing sex with children, grandchildren, and cousins.

Laws being laws and people being people, sex with children in the family remained quite common. The Renaissance of the fourteenth century, an era celebrated for its humanist morality, attempted to ban child sexual abuse, with little apparent success. Providing some clarifying legislation, a sixteenth-century British jury ruled that girls could consent to sex at ten years old and marry at age twelve. Sex with a nine-year-old girl was a felony; sex with a ten- to twelve-year-old a misdemeanor.

When they founded the Plymouth Colony in 1620, the Pilgrims brought their confused ideology, now known as Puritanism, and the European tradition of hanging witches with them. In 1672, a Connecticut father who was found guilty of sexually molesting his daughter was executed. Lest anyone believe that his daughter was his innocent victim, she was sentenced to a whipping for her part in the crime.

Social critic H. L. Mencken defined Puritanism as "The haunting fear that someone, somewhere, may be happy." Later, he added, "The objection to Puritans is not that they try to make us think as they do, but that they try to make us do as they think."

Mencken had a point. Following their effort to "purify" the Church of England, the Puritans went on to "purify"—or condemn to eternal sexual hypocrisy, depending on one's point of view—the nascent United States. Having traveled to the new world in search of religious tolerance, the Puritans imposed a slew of highly intolerant rules when they arrived.

Salem (a word that's hard to say without adding its adjunct, "witch hunt") was ripe. For months, the colony had no governor, no government, and no laws. Its citizens lived under constant threat, real or imagined, of attack by French Canadians and Native Americans. Unaccustomed to growing food in New England's harsh climate and rocky soil, the colonists were hungry, too. During the long, dark winter of 1692, Salem was wracked by political, economic, and social instability—the same scenario that would lay the groundwork for the rise of German Nazism nearly three centuries later.

The stage was set for a crisis, and in the winter of 1692, when several village girls began behaving strangely—barking and growling, crawling and choking—a minister pronounced the girls "bewitched." The diagnosis set Salem's smoldering demonology on fire, and sparked the first recorded episode of American mass hysteria.

"When life is too confusing," wrote Mark Pendergrast in his 1991 book, *Victims of Memory*, "a scapegoat helps, whether it be a witch, a Jew, a Communist, or a pedophile." Scapegoating did indeed help justify Salem's satanic panic. It also proved lethal for the nineteen innocent citizens of Salem who were executed for "bewitching" young girls, and left its indelible stain on the not-yet United States.

In the first American schools, teachers recommended that children be clothed when in the presence of adults, even their own parents, to protect them from their elders' lust. Apparently that failed to do the trick. In 1877, the American Humane Association was founded to protect two at-risk populations: animals and abused children.

By the turn of the twentieth century, American child welfare organizations had identified incest as the most common form of child sexual abuse.

Enter Freud.

On April 21, 1896, forty-year-old Sigmund Freud delivered his first major address, "The Aetiology of Hysteria," to the Vienna Society for Psychiatry and Neurology. In it he reported that more than a dozen of his patients were suffering from a strange array of symptoms: nervousness, insomnia, irritability, loss of appetite for food or sex, and "a tendency to cause trouble." In each case, Freud said, he'd traced the patient's symptoms to childhood sexual abuse.

Later that year, Freud announced that he'd uncovered repressed memories of early childhood sexual abuse in *every one* of his patients. Writing to his close friend and colleague Dr. Wilhelm Fliess, Freud identified unconscious memories of infantile sexual abuse as the source of most if not all mental ills. Citing a patient's memory of being raped by her father at age two, he proposed that psychoanalysts adopt "a new motto" that would return to therapists' lips one hundred years later: "What has been done to you, poor child?"

The response to Freud's "seduction theory" was swift and brutal. Three weeks after he presented "The Aetiology of Hysteria," Freud wrote to Fleiss, "My consulting room is empty, that for weeks on end I see no new faces."

By the following September, Freud was in the throes of creeping doubt. "Let me tell you straight away the great secret which has been slowly dawning on me in recent months," he confided to Fleiss. "I no longer believe in my 'neurotica,' or seduction theory. . . . [I]t was hardly credible that perverted acts against children were so general."

For the next six years, though, Freud kept his doubts to himself, suffering the wrath of his peers, a group that seems, in retrospect, a bit short on both consciousness and compassion. Case in point: German psychoanalyst Karl Abraham. Once Freud's star pupil, Abraham acknowledged that many of his female patients had undisputed memories of incestuous rape, as Freud had said. Abraham blamed the girls' "seductiveness" for the abuse. The molestation, he claimed, "Was desired by the child unconsciously [because of an] abnormal psycho-sexual constitution."

By 1901, Freud was a desperate, lonely, discredited man, seemingly in need of some good therapy. "I will make no further attempts to break through my isolation, " he wrote to Fleiss. "The time is otherwise bleak, outstandingly bleak." Nonetheless, bravely—or masochistically—Freud was still defending his seduction theory in 1917.

"You must not suppose, . . ." he wrote, "that sexual abuse of a child by its nearest male relatives belongs entirely to the realm of phantasy. Most analysts will have treated cases in which such events were real and could be unimpeachably established."

Supporters of Freud's original stance say that isolation drove Freud to abandon his beliefs about the prevalence of child sexual abuse. Opponents say he finally recognized the truth. In either case, the world's most renowned expert on the human mind seemed to have trouble making up his own. In 1933, Freud went public with the retraction that would alter the course of psychotherapeutic history—and would silence incest victims for generations to come.

"Almost all my women patients told me that they had been seduced by their father," he wrote. "I was driven to recognize in the end that these reports were untrue and so came to understand that hysterical symptoms were derived from phantasy and not real occurrences."

Along with his "discovery" of the unconscious mind and the slip named in his honor, Freud is perhaps best known for the Oedipus complex, the theory he substituted for his seduction theory. Initially he believed that only little boys experienced sexual desire for their opposite-sex parents. Later he promoted the notion that girls, too, desired their fathers and therefore wanted to kill their mothers.

"It is the fate of all of us, perhaps," Freud wrote, "to direct our first sexual impulse towards our mother and our first hatred and our first murderous wish against our father."

Reading this, I remembered the recurring nightmare that had haunted me since I was a small girl, the dream that sparked the persistent insomnia that plagued me as a child, the dream that was in my nighttime rotation still. *The police are chasing me. I'm running as fast as I can, ducking into alleyways, sprinting up endless flights of stairs. But I know I'm going to get caught, and I know that I deserve to be. After all, I've killed my own mother.*

Focused on Freud, I started noticing how often his name came up. Seventy years after Freud's reversal, *The New York Times* was still debating the causes and consequences of this "momentous turning point in the history of psychoanalysis."

The New York Times
August 25, 1981
"Did Freud's Isolation Lead Him to Reverse Theory on Neurosis?"

"Why oh why couldn't Freud believe his own ears?" Dr. Karl Menninger wrote. . . . "Why did he knuckle under to those who said, 'Oh, people don't do those dreadful things to children.' They are still saying that, just as some people say there was no holocaust, is no torture, etc."

This view won some surprising endorsement recently from a prominent Freud archivist, Dr. Jeffrey Moussiaeff Masson, a Berkeley psychoanalyst selected by Anna Freud as director of the project to publish her father's complete letters for the first time.

Coming on top of Krafft-Ebing's disdainful characterization of the seduction theory as "a scientific fairy tale," Dr. Masson said, "it was simply too much for Freud. He retreated."

—*Ralph Blumenthal*

Working with Roselyn gave me access to experts in the field, including the controversial Freud scholar Jeffrey Masson. He agreed to a phone interview.

"Freud was a brave man for a short time," Masson told me. "He was perhaps the first person in history to take seriously the different ways in which children could be hurt in their early life. He alerted us to the importance of childhood sexual abuse, an important truth that had never been recognized.

"Later, he retracted his earlier comments about the reality of abuse. The world has been divided ever since between those who believe he was right the first time and those who believe he was right the second time."

"Why did Freud recant?" I asked.

"His colleagues couldn't face the true prevalence of incest. They frightened him into giving up his belief."

Ironically, Freud's history repeated itself in Masson's. In 1980, Masson completed his study of Freud's writings and publicly concluded that Freud had "capitulated to reactionary forces in society that wanted sexual abuse kept hidden." Immediately, the same traditional psychoanalytic world that had ousted Freud ousted Masson, firing him from his job as director of the Freud Archives. Masson's membership in the International Psychoanalytical Association was revoked. And he became a hero to feminist scholars, including Roselyn Taylor.

Masson said he regrets nothing. "For the past hundred years, Freudian analysts have believed that women who say they've been abused are just fantasizing. They believe that real abuse hardly ever happens.

"But children are still being sexually assaulted. Grown women who remember being abused and report it to their psychiatrists are still disbelieved. For far too long these women have been labeled mentally ill or unbalanced or as having too great an imagination, when all they were doing was telling the truth.

"There was no awareness of child sexual abuse in America until feminist activists like Florence Rush, Judith Herman, and Diana Russell came along."

By the 1920s, U.S. sociologists had concluded that many delin-
quent girls were victims of sexual abuse and that in most cases,
family members were to blame. Their findings briefly replaced
the stereotype of the molester as a predatory stranger lurking in
the shadows, preying on the temptress child. But soon the repercussions of Freud's reversal rippled across the ocean. Like a child
taking candy from a stranger, Americans eagerly swallowed the
notion that "phantasies," not incestuous abuse, were responsible
for most incest claims.

By the 1940s, incest had regained its reputation as a one-in-a
million occurrence. Heeding the advice of psychiatrists, the
American Bar Association warned judges that women and children often lied about sexual abuse. Even among social workers,
allegations of incest were increasingly disbelieved.

Enter Dr. Alfred Kinsey. In 1953, the "father of sexology"
published *Sexual Behavior in the Human Female*. This first com-
prehensive study of female sexuality was blasted, banned, and,
most of all, bought. Sales of the tome were, well, explosive.

Sexual Behavior in the Human Female contained a finding that
should have made headlines but didn't. One-quarter of the
women interviewed by the Kinsey team reported having had, in
childhood, "Undesired sexual contact or experience with an
adult man." Not to worry, Kinsey reassured the populace: a child's
sexual activity would prepare her for better sexual adjustment
later in life. Jailing the offender, he said, leaving his family des-
titute and his children wards of the court, would do the children
more harm than good.

The following year, Vladimir Nabokov published *Lolita*, the
story of an older man sexually obsessed with his twelve-year-old
stepdaughter. The novel provoked widespread moral outrage and
runaway sales.

In 1962, the Roman Catholic Church published its own
treatise on the subject. Without acknowledging the prevalence
of the problem, *On the Manner of Proceeding in Cases of the Crime*

of Solicitation established protocols for dioceses dealing with a priest who "tempts a penitent . . . in the act of sacramental confession . . . towards impure or obscene matters."

Investigations and trials of these priests were to be conducted in secrecy; their outcomes were never to be disclosed. Bishops were advised to pursue these cases "in the most secretive way . . . restrained by a perpetual silence . . . and everyone is to observe the strictest secret, which is commonly regarded as a secret of the Holy Office . . . under the penalty of excommunication."

In 1961, Dr. Henry Kempe, a thirty-nine-year-old Jewish pediatrician who had escaped Nazi Germany as a teenager, named a syndrome and shattered the myth that parents were incapable of hurting their own children.

Initially Kempe's battered-child syndrome was received by his peers with as much enthusiasm as Freud's seduction theory was by his. But over the next few years, evidence began to trump denial.

Time Magazine
July 20, 1962
"Medicine: Battered-Child Syndrome"

To many doctors, the incident is becoming distressingly familiar. A child, usually under three, is brought to the office with multiple fractures—often including a fractured skull. The parents express appropriate concern, report that the baby fell out of bed, or tumbled down the stairs, or was injured by a playmate. But X-rays and experience lead the doctor to a different conclusion: the child has been beaten by his parents. He is suffering from what last week's A.M.A. Journal calls "the battered-child syndrome."

As pediatricians learned to recognize the signs of physical abuse, they also discovered symptoms of sexual abuse. Starting with California, one state after another passed laws mandating doctors, mental health care workers, teachers, social workers, day-care providers, and law enforcement personnel to report cases of suspected physical, emotional, or sexual abuse. In 1969, the Children's Division of the American Humane Association conducted one of the first studies that explored not only the incidence of child sexual abuse but also the lasting emotional trauma it causes.

Which is not to say that the dragon of denial had been slain. Also in 1969, the *Georgia Law Review* wrote, "Child molestation is a relatively minor crime. [The] absurdity of enforcing most of our sex laws should be obvious, even to the most prudish Neo-Puritans. And child molesters should be released on probation or after paying a small fine if they didn't use physical force."

Later that year, Mario Biaggi, Democratic congressman from the Bronx, became the first legislator to argue for child sexual abuse legislation. Citing a new poll that ranked child sexual abuse among the nation's three most pressing problems, Biaggi urged immediate action. It took five years, but on January 31, 1974, President Nixon signed the Child Abuse Prevention and Treatment Act (CAPTA) into law.

Sponsored by Senator Walter Mondale, CAPTA provided federal matching funds to states that established child abuse detection, prosecution, and prevention programs.

Enter feminism.

In April 1971, exactly seventy-five years after Freud presented his seduction theory in Vienna, psychiatric social worker Florence Rush addressed the New York Radical Feminists' Rape Conference, criticizing Freud for having retracted it.

Rush based her speech on her work with molested children at the New York Society for the Prevention of Cruelty to Children. "The violent rapist and the boyfriend/husband are one," she said.

In 1980, Rush clarified her remarks in *The Best Kept Secret: Sexual Abuse of Children*, a shocker of a book laced with gripping testimonies. Child sexual abuse continues today, Rush wrote, because it has always been, and still is, condoned by society— a conclusion that would have seemed outrageous to me before I began my research, but seemed perfectly obvious now.

As Rush was speaking, a social worker on the opposite coast was tackling the same problem from the opposite point of view. Henry Giarretto, a sixty-year-old psychologist in San Jose, California, also treated sexually abused adults and children. Like Kinsey, though, Giarretto argued that the prevailing treatment plan for incestuous families—incarcerating the fathers, treating only the child victims—ruined not only the perpetrators' lives but also the lives of their wives and children. Incestuous fathers could and should be rehabilitated, he said, their wives and kids provided with financial and legal assistance as well as therapy. After a period of judicial and therapeutic supervision, assuming that the wives and children agreed, he recommended that the fathers be reunited with their families.

Feminist experts protested that no child could ever be safe with a man who had molested her. Nonetheless, Giarretto's Child Sexual Abuse Treatment Program (CSATP) was launched in Santa Clara County in 1971. Giarretto and his wife, Anna, founded the family treatment component of the program, Parents United. Over the next several years, more than seventy programs throughout the United States and Canada were built on the CSATP model.

In my pile of books, I found two sexual abuse memoirs, both published in 1980.

Daddy's Girl
1980

"Daddy, are we bad?"

"Course not."

"And you really mean it, this is what all little girls and their daddies do?"

"Didn't I tell you that?"

"You love me, Daddy?"

"What the hell kinda question's that? Course I do. Nobody'll ever love you better than your old man."

"I love you, too. Wouldn't it be fun to tell . . . ?"

"No, no! We're not telling anybody, are we?"

"Oh, no. I can keep secrets better than anyone."

"That's my girl."

. . . I wanted to tell mother the truth and considered the idea very carefully. But before I arrived at the actual decision to confide in her, Daddy became alarmingly descriptive and specific in his threats.

"Don't you ever tell anyone, ever!" That ominous little drum beat away in his temple. "You want me to go to prison? They'd put you away, too. You want to go to jail? Do you?"

So now I knew he'd lied about everything. Other fathers and daughters didn't do the things we did. Well and truly terrified, I swore never to tell.

—Charlotte Vale Allen, Simon & Schuster

Michelle Remembers was coauthored by Canadian psychiatrist Lawrence Pazder and Michelle Smith, the patient who later became his wife. The book introduced a new phrase into the lexicon: *satanic ritual abuse.*

During the course of six hundred hypnosis sessions, Pazder wrote, he'd helped Smith remember the satanic rituals she was forced to attend as a child.

part two

1983–1993

There was a little girl
Who had a little curl
Right in the middle of her forehead.
And when she was good
She was very, very good.
And when she was bad
She was horrid.

—Henry Wadsworth Longfellow

three

Please Question Your Child (and Your Childhood)

Dear Parent:

This Department is conducting a criminal
investigation involving child molestation. . . .
Please question your child to see if he or she has
been a witness to any crime or if he or she has
been a victim. . . .

—*Harry L. Kuhlmeyer Jr., chief of police,
Manhattan Beach, California, September 8, 1983*

Roselyn was right. My transformation from nuclear missile collaborator to incest-book editor was not without complications.

The more I learned about child sexual abuse, the more I felt I'd joined a back-room club whose secret password was "the ugly truth." Doing my research was like examining X-rays of the nuclear family and finding cancer in every cell.

By day I changed diapers and edited the testimonies of convicted child molesters, praised my sons' finger paintings and transcribed interviews with sodomized little girls. By night I read *Goodnight, Moon* to my beautiful boys and then turned to my own bedtime reading: *Conspiracy of Silence, Father-Daughter Incest, Betrayal of Innocence.*

Then there was the matter of my marriage.

Doing time in my Silicon Valley cubicle, I told myself what the save-your-marriage books promised: if I got myself a more fulfilling life, I'd be a more fulfilled wife. But after months of fulfilling work with Roselyn, my relationship with Robert was still sliding. My self-help campaign felt more like self-hype.

My situation called for a new and different happy-ending story, so I told myself one. When I was done with Roselyn's book, we'd send the kids to my brother's house for a long weekend and take a romantic getaway. I'd forget about the terrible things I'd spent the past months learning. Robert and I would get to know and love and lust after each other again.

But then I cashed my last check from Roselyn and realized that I was hooked. How could I spend my time researching B&Bs or shopping for peek-a-boo lingerie when somewhere in America, a little girl—actually three out of ten little girls—were being sexually abused? I returned the romantic-escape guidebooks to the library, wrote a pitch for an incest article, and sent it to twenty national and local magazines.

Time Magazine
September 5, 1983
"Child Abuse: The Ultimate Betrayal"

...The number of reported cases of child abuse in the U.S. is rising sharply. . . . While alarmed by those trends, most analysts see a glimmer of hope in the grim statistics.

They believe that the figures may reflect a growing alertness and willingness among officials in schools, hospitals, law-enforcement and social agencies to detect and report instances of child abuse. Relatives and neighbors of the victims also seem more ready to ask the relevant local authorities to intervene.

The wall of silence is breaking down even in cases of incest and sexual abuse of children by close acquaintances, which were almost always hushed up in the past.

—*Ed Magnuson, Meg Grant, and James Wilde*

If *Time Magazine* gets it, I thought, could an assignment be far behind?

Sure enough, I got a call from the editor of *West*, the Sunday magazine of the *San Jose Mercury-News*. He was intrigued, he said, but dubious. "No one will believe that incest happens as often as you say it does," he said, "unless you put a human face on the issue. And where are you going to find an incest victim who's willing to go public?"

The next day I climbed the sagging front steps of a three-story, faded-beauty Victorian in downtown San Jose—the headquarters of Parents United (PU), the incest treatment clinic dedicated to family reunification, which happened to be located a couple of miles from my house.

The receptionist sent me to the director's office, where a slight, impish-looking man with a shock of snowy hair and a Dali moustache materialized from behind the teetering pile of folders on his desk. "I'm Hank Giarretto," he greeted me with an ear-to-ear grin and an outstretched hand.

I told Giarretto what I was looking for: an incestuous family whose story, witnessed and recorded by me, would tell the bigger one. "We don't see a lot of reporters around here," Giarretto said, leaning forward in his seat. "I'm wondering—is this a personal issue for you?"

The nerve of him, I thought, and I opened my mouth to say no. "That's not why I'm here," I heard myself saying instead.

"I see," Giarretto said. After an awkward silence, he said that if I'd agree to safeguard his clients' anonymity, he'd try to find me a family to profile.

Giarretto stood and shook my hand, holding it a beat too long. "I hope you get what you need," he said.

A couple of days later, I got a call from Angela Gotti, a Parents United therapist in training. Angela was treating a family she asked me to call the Rands. In hopes of helping other families in their situation, she said, the Rands had agreed to let me observe their sessions with her.

"Jim and Sandy met in high school," Angela said. "Rachel, the oldest of their three daughters, was born while Sandy was still in school.

"A year ago, when the girls were eleven, thirteen, and seventeen, they came to Sandy and told her that their father had been raping all three of them for the past several years. Jim went to jail for nine months. We started working with him when he was released.

"Jim was physically and sexually abused as a child. The same thing's true of most of the incest perpetrators we see. That's why treating these fathers is so important. Dealing with childhood abuse doesn't just help the kids of this generation. It breaks the cycle for generations to come."

I remembered what Roselyn Taylor had told me about the PU philosophy: "To say that incest occurs because its perpetrators were molested as children doesn't address the fact that the vast majority of molesters are men."

"Why do so few abused women abuse their children?" Roselyn had said. "The main cause of incest isn't incest, but the predatory sexuality that men have been conditioned into, along with the economic and social power they wield over women and children."

"If Jim finishes the program here," Angela was saying, "and if he convinces his probation officer, the judge, his therapists, and his wife and daughters that his rehabilitation is complete, he'll stay out of prison.

"Whether or not he captures the brass ring and goes back to his family . . ." She shrugged. "That'll be up to them."

"Come in," Angela called out in response to my knock on the door of her basement office.

Mother, father, and twelve-year-old Sarah Rand were lined up on the weary plaid couch, staring straight ahead like strangers traveling together on a train. Fourteen-year-old Lisa was slumped onto a brown metal folding chair, eighteen-year-old Rachel perched rigidly on another. Angela Gotti was squeezed into a child-size armchair, her grandmotherly bulk overflowing its bounds.

There was no seventh seat in this closet of an office, and no room for one. So I sank cross-legged onto the floor, back against the wall, Bic pen and steno pad in hand.

"Will someone tell Meredith why we're here?" Angela asked.

They inhabited their seats and their bodies stiffly, these Rands: chess pieces awaiting reconfiguration when the next move was made. But who would make it? The only sound in the room was the muted hum of rush-hour traffic, punctuated by the metronome tick-tock of the institutional, blank-faced clock on the wall.

Rachel surveyed her sisters. Lisa, the middle child, pulled her chair so close to her father's place on the couch that her knees, incredibly—*how can she*—were touching his. Among the girls there was a ducking of heads, a fluttering of eyes: permission granted.

Rachel leaned forward, immaculate white Adidas planted flat on the floor, nail-bitten fingers gripping acid-washed-blue-jean knees.

"I'm the one who told on Dad," she said. "So I'll say how it happened."

She turned her head to glare at her father, who met her eyes, a sorrowful expression on his chiseled, clean-shaven face. Jim Rand looked too young to be the father of three teenage daughters, and too handsome to be married to Sandy, the overweight, graying woman seated at the opposite end of the couch, as far from her husband as she could get.

"Go on, sweetheart," Angela prompted Rachel.

"I *will*," Rachel snapped. She gathered up her long black mane with one hand, twisted it into a spiky knot with the other.

"Before I told on him," Rachel began, "my dad had been molesting me for ten years. I knew it was wrong because he always said it was our little secret. But he swore he'd go to jail if I told.

"I loved my dad more than anyone. And my little sisters needed him. I didn't want him to go to jail. But I was afraid he'd start doing it to them. So I promised not to tell on him if he promised not to touch my sisters."

Twin spots of color bloomed on Sandy's cheeks. Sarah, the baby of the family, climbed into her mother's lap. I watched Jim, who was watching Rachel. As she spoke his jaw tightened; his forehead furrowed. Slowly, deliberately, he uncrossed his legs.

As if responding to a hypnotist's cue, Rachel's eyelids drooped; her body swayed toward his. Then she jerked herself upright. Her big, black eyes—mirror images of her father's—sparked and flashed. Intercepting the crossfire, Sandy squeezed her eyes shut.

"He swore I was the only one," Rachel continued, "so I learned to cope. I separated my self from my body. I told myself it was just my body lying there on that bed. My dad would never do those things to the real me.

"At first, I'd be upset for weeks every time he molested me. Near the end I'd gotten to where he'd finish and I'd get up and forget about it within an hour or two. Then one day I heard Sarah crying in her room." Rachel looked at her youngest sister. "I just knew why. I felt like my heart was on fire. I opened her door and lay down next to her and asked her what was wrong."

Across the room, the twelve-year-old wrapped her arms around her mother's neck. "Sarah," Angela said, "you know we can stop this any time you want. This session, this whole process, is for you and your sisters. Not for your parents. Not for the reporter. For you."

"I want Rachel to tell," Sarah whispered.

Her oldest sister exhaled a ragged breath. "Sarah didn't want to admit what was happening to her, because Dad had told her *she* was the only one," Rachel said. "But finally she admitted that Dad had been . . . handling her, too."

Sarah had nearly disappeared into her mother's body. Lisa's knees were pressed together, one foot spasmodically tapping the floor. Through clenched teeth, Rachel persevered.

"When Sarah got home that day, Lisa and I talked to her. That's when we found out that Dad had been molesting all three of us since we were little."

Jim leaned forward. "It hurts deep down to face up to what I've done to you," he croaks. "I'm so sorry. I—"

"I don't accept your apology," Rachel interrupted him. "You can sit here and talk about facing up to it. Well, we face up to it whether we want to or not. Do you know that Sarah still wakes up screaming every night? Do you know that Lisa lost her baby-sitting job because the parents found out why you were in jail? You just make me feel guilty with all your damn apologies. I don't want to hear them anymore."

Except for Rachel, all the Rands were crying now. Even Angela's eyes were wet. I was near tears myself. Four thousand children had been treated at Parents United in the thirteen years of its existence. Angela had treated several dozen of them. How did she come to work every day? How did she leave scenes like this behind when she went home at night?

"Now you see how it is for us," Rachel told me. "I want you to write it all down. I want every kid who's being molested right now to know that they shouldn't keep it a secret. And I want every man out there to know what it does to children to be sexually abused."

Rachel looked at Sarah, then at Lisa, then at me. "If we can keep this from happening to just one girl or one boy," she choked out, "maybe all this pain will be worth it."

I swallowed hard. "I'll do what I can," I promised.

The day I signed up to edit Roselyn's book I took on a mission: hers. Now it was mine, and it was engulfing me, a snowball tumbling down a mountain, gaining momentum as it grew.

I found it all endlessly compelling: the newest incest study, the latest theory, the most promising new treatment. I talked about it with my editor at *West* magazine, with the experts I interviewed, and with Roselyn and her colleagues, to whom I turned for reality checks.

Conversations with my husband and with my friends seemed trivial in comparison. While I was debating which carpet to buy, or whether my best friend should break up with her boyfriend, some child's father was doing to her what Jim Rand had done to his.

Years ago, I'd witnessed a gruesome car accident and its aftermath. I'd never described it to anyone, loath to unload that memory on anyone lucky enough to have been elsewhere on that sunny, bloody day. I felt the same way about my days at PU. I didn't want to impose the scenes in my head on the people I loved. But keeping my experiences at PU from them was making me feel a little bit crazy, and very much alone.

When I came home at night and Robert asked, "How was your day?" I knew he was being half-sarcastic, half-hopeful that my answer would paint a sheen of normality over our life. I wished I could give him what he wanted and deserved: a cheerful travelogue, a pithy sociological tale. But a different movie was playing in my head. "Fine," I would say.

I tried to tell myself that the deepening division between Robert and me was normal, busy-parents-of-small-children stuff. I knew that the line I'd drawn down the center of my life wasn't helping, but I was afraid that if I asked him my most pressing question—*How can men do these things?*—I wouldn't be able to keep from asking the next.

How can I trust you, sleep with you, love you, knowing that men do these things?

I'd been doing some freelance editing for a small feminist press. The publisher invited me to a conference in Dallas to help staff her booth. Robert had a caged bird on his hands, and he knew it. "Go," he said.

It was fun. I missed my sons, but my body felt light and floating outside the reach of their sticky little hands. I met people, women mostly. Lesbians mostly. We went to dinner each night in huge messy groups at eight or nine or ten o'clock. We drank beers and talked and argued and laughed: smart, interesting, grown-up stuff.

On the first night, I sat across the table from Jane, an androgynous woman who looked like a cute boy. Unlike most of the other lesbians I'd met, she didn't change the subject when I told her about my kids. She asked to see pictures, and when she saw them her blue eyes lit up. She wanted to know everything about them. She looked at me and then at their pictures and then back at me.

"He has your eyes," she said, her long, thin finger tracing Matthew's profile.

"He has your smile," she said, smiling at the picture of Charlie.

Jane lived near Boston. She used to work at a day-care center, she said. She missed being around kids.

I felt oddly flustered. "I thought lesbians didn't like children," I blurted with characteristic tact.

"Oh, no!" Jane covered her mouth with her hand, pantomiming surprise. "I must be straight."

I hope not, I thought. And then I saw that Jane was smiling at me, and then I was smiling at her, and then she was laughing— but with me, not at me. *She's so kind*, I thought, *and I'm such a dork*, and I started laughing too.

The next day, Jane hung out at my booth. That night we sat together at dinner again, and the night after that.

I snuck peeks at Jane as we were breaking down our booths. I noticed that she was sneaking peeks back. Standing outside the convention center, waiting for our shuttles, we exchanged addresses and promised to write. She hugged me good-bye. I felt the tips of her breasts against mine. My knees actually quivered. *What the hell was* that *about*, I asked myself, not wanting to know.

Back home in my real life, I was riveted to a story unfolding in Manhattan Beach, California. The mother of a boy who attended the McMartin Preschool had accused a teacher named Ray Buckey of sodomizing her two-and-a-half-year-old son.

Buckey had been arrested. In my morning paper I read the letter that the chief of police had sent to the parents of the school's two hundred toddlers.

Letter to McMartin Preschool Parents
September 8, 1983

Dear Parent:

This Department is conducting a criminal investigation involving child molestation. . . .

Please question your child to see if he or she has been a witness to any crime or if he or she has been a victim. Our investigation indicates that possible criminal acts include: oral sex, fondling of genitals, buttock or chest area, and sodomy, possibly committed under the pretense of "taking the child's temperature."

Also photos may have been taken of children without their clothing. Any information from your child regarding having ever observed Ray Buckey to leave a classroom alone with a child during any nap period, or if they have ever observed Ray Buckey tie up a child, is important.

. . . Please do not discuss this investigation with anyone outside your immediate family. Do not contact or discuss the investigation with Raymond Buckey, any member of the accused defendant's family, or employees connected with the McMartin Pre-School.

—*Harry L. Kuhlmeyer Jr., chief of police, Manhattan Beach, California*

According to news reports, the district attorney had hired social workers to interview the students. The interviewers had used hand puppets and anatomically correct dolls to help the children describe what had happened to them. The consultants had concluded that dozens, maybe hundreds of McMartin students had been sexually abused.

Incredibly, a similar story was being reported from the small town of Jordan, Minnesota. A mother had accused James Rud, a neighbor who sometimes babysat her son and daughter, of sexually abusing both kids. Rud had confessed and implicated other adults in the town. Dozens of children were saying that they too had been molested—by Rud, by a local preacher, by their own parents. Twenty-six children had been removed from their homes. Twenty-four adults had been charged with hundreds of sex crimes against children.

Monsters, I thought. *These men are monsters.*

Robert found me huddled under a blanket on the couch, transfixed by *Something About Amelia*, a made-for-TV movie starring Ted Danson as an affluent father who'd finally been caught molesting his teenage daughter, Amelia. Glen Close played his clueless, wide-eyed wife.

"Don't you get enough of this craziness all day?" Robert said. "Why don't you take a break?"

"I will," I mumbled.

But I wouldn't, I knew.

There weren't nearly enough of us who understood what was happening to children in their own homes. If we took a break, who'd save all those kids?

Something About Amelia broke TV viewing records for 1984 and went on to earn two Golden Globes, three Emmys, and a nomination for the 1984 Humanitas Prize.

Phil Donahue, in characteristic trailblazing fashion, devoted an episode of his show to fathers who'd molested their daughters.

"I thought I was doing her a favor," one incestuous father explained.

"I'm a decent man," said another. "I provide for my family. I don't run around on my wife, and I've never slept with anyone except my wife and my daughters."

The audience responded, as the transcript described it, with "sounds of remonstrance, disbelief."

Parents United allowed me to observe each of the Rands in each of his or her individual and group therapy sessions. As a journalist, I couldn't have asked for better access. As a human being, I was finding it to be the hardest deal I'd ever kept.

If tonight is Tuesday, it must be Perpetrators' Group, I thought as I walked into a big, bland, fluorescently lit group room before the men arrived. I draped my jacket over the back of a brown metal folding chair, opened my notebook, and planted my feet on the indoor-outdoor-carpeted floor.

At precisely 7 P.M., Jim Rand and fourteen other men shuffled in and settled into their chairs. The members of this group were so diverse—young, middle-aged, and old; white, black, Filipino, and Latino; some with automotive grease under their fingernails, others with pocket-protectors protruding from their button-down shirts—it was hard to believe they had anything in common. But they did, of course. Each of them had sexually abused a child, or several children.

"We have a reporter with us tonight," announced John Singleton, the therapist in training who ran the group, ducking his head at me. In a normal therapy group, the therapist would be obligated to ask his clients' permission to be observed by a journalist. But this was no normal therapy group, and these clients had relinquished their right to privacy as a condition of their treatment here.

"Let's get started." John called on a middle-aged black man in a baby-blue velour tracksuit. "Lloyd. Why don't you go first?"

Lloyd's eyes were fixed on the floor. "I crossed the line with my granddaughter," he mumbled.

"How?" John asked.

Lloyd's knees jerked. His navy-blue Nikes tapped the floor. "It wasn't my fault," he said. "I *told* her to stop prancing around the house in baby-doll pajamas. She wouldn't listen."

A young Filipino man with a slicked-back pompadour leaned forward in his chair, nodding vigorously. "They don't understand. A man has needs," he said. "My wife gained fifty pounds after she had the girls. What was I *supposed* to do?"

Groans erupted from several of the men in the room, including Jim Rand. "Can anyone answer that question?" Singleton asked above the dull roar.

"The molest was your responsibility," Jim said, using the word "molest" as a noun, as everyone at PU did. "Not your granddaughter's." Jim turned to the young man with the tall hair. "Not your wife's."

Watching Jim, I wondered, as I always did, *Am I witnessing a man in the process of genuine self-improvement? Or a con man simulating remorse to get his wife and daughters to take him back, and his therapists to keep him out of jail?*

"You have to care about what's good for your kids," said a middle-aged white man in an expensive-looking suit. "More than you care about what feels good to you.

"When my daughter turned fifteen and started dating other men," he continued, "I became insanely jealous. Her boyfriend came to pick her up one night. The next thing I knew I had my hands around his throat. If my wife hadn't pulled me off of him, I would have killed him. That's how the molest came out."

As the man spoke, I heard another voice in my head. It was my father's voice, and he was yelling. I was fifteen and my father was yelling at Carl, my first boyfriend, telling him to go away.

I saw my father in the doorway of our apartment. The veins in his forehead were throbbing, bulging blue.

No. I was standing behind him. He was blocking the door, keeping me from Carl. I couldn't have seen the veins on his forehead.

"Stay away from her," my father shouted, "or I'll call the police!" He grabbed Carl by the shoulders and shook him, hard. "She's mine! I'll kill you if you don't leave her alone."

The memory blurred, retreating from reach. I willed it back. *This is something I need to know.*

And then I saw *Carl* yelling, *Carl's* face contorted with rage. *Carl* shouting, "She's mine. I'll kill you if you don't leave her alone."

Which version was real? Who was the violent one, the one who'd called me his?

My father?

My boyfriend?

Both of them?

My father often lost his temper. He'd slapped me in the face more than once.

Carl had done those things, too.

Had that fight even happened? Was I making the whole thing up?

I knew my father. He wouldn't have threatened the boy I loved.

Then why had I left home at age seventeen?

"It's common for fathers who have sexually abused their daughters, physically or emotionally, to explode when their daughters begin to direct their sexual attentions elsewhere," John Singleton was saying. I wrote that down, underlining the words <u>physically or emotionally</u>.

And then I stopped taking notes and looked around at the men who were sitting in their rigid chairs denying and confessing the abuse they'd inflicted on the children who trusted them.

"See you next week," Singleton said. Around me, the men were shrugging into their jackets, folding up their metal chairs.

"Can I get that for you?" The man in the three-piece suit was standing over me, pointing at my chair. I grabbed my briefcase and speed-walked out of the building, then locked myself into my car.

My hands were shaking as I turned the key in the ignition. I told myself I'd feel better when I got home.

I let myself into my quiet kitchen, yellow daisies dancing up the kelly-green-papered walls, Revereware copper pans gleaming on their cast-iron hooks. I stood at the sink, staring at my boys' crusty Peter Rabbit bowls and Sesame Street sippy cups, the detritus of the family dinner I'd missed. Slushy puddles of instant mashed potatoes. Shreds of the pot roast I'd left for Robert to heat up. A few stray frozen peas. A flash of anger ran through me. How many decades of "post-feminism" would have to pass before husbands started cooking fresh vegetables?

And then standing there in my suburban kitchen, I started crying, and I couldn't stop.

Robert appeared in the doorway, ice cream spoon in hand, eyes wide and worried. He dropped his spoon into the sink and put his arms around me. Our relationship had been hurting for months, or was it years now? But for the first time in ten years of marriage, my body involuntarily recoiled from his touch.

"What's wrong?" he asked.

"It's about my father," I choked out.

"What about him?"

"It's about my father," I said again.

Robert told me to come to bed, but I couldn't go there with him. I cried myself to sleep on the couch.

As a middle-class, New York Jewish 1950s child with an impressive panoply of neurotic symptoms—mysterious rashes, spiking fevers, hemorrhaging nosebleeds, a howling fear of the dark—I'd spent more than my share of fifty-minute-hours in the tufted-leather offices of the psychiatrists, child psychologists, and

Rorschach-test administrators my parents had hired to cure me. When I left home for good, my symptoms had miraculously disappeared. The farce and the failure of the treatment had left me with a sour taste for the couch.

But if I was going to raise my children in the happy family I'd promised them before they were conceived, Robert and I needed help. In suburban San Jose in 1984, wise elders and shamanic healers were in short supply.

There *was* one therapist I knew who did more than murmur and nod. Angela Gotti wasn't an overpaid, unfeeling automaton. She cared about her clients; I'd seen her cry real tears. And compared to the marital issues she dealt with at Parents United, mine and Robert's would be a piece of cake.

Any traditional therapist would have refused to treat a reporter who was writing an investigative article that featured her. But that was one of the things I liked about Angela. She was an Italian, Roman Catholic grandmother, but her therapeutic approach was as far from traditional as the Vatican was from the Lower East Side.

On Thursday morning at nine, Robert and I knocked at the door of a ranch-style tract house just like ours, a few blocks from ours. Angela hugged me and then Robert, led us into the semiconverted garage that doubled as her home office, and waved us onto vinyl beanbag chairs. She sank into a beat-up pleather recliner.

"Tell me why you're here," she began.

Vinyl squeaked and beans shifted as Robert and I avoided each other's eyes.

"What I want to know," Angela coaxed us, "is what it is you're hoping for."

After another long silence, I said the one thing I was sure of: "I don't want to put my kids through a divorce."

Where had I heard those words before? From my mother, of course. As a teenager flush with the arrogance of young love, I kept telling my mother that she should divorce my dad. Each time, my mother shrugged and told me—I'm paraphrasing, but not much—that they were staying together for the sake of the kids.

She made good on her vow. She didn't leave my father until approximately five seconds after my younger brother left home and came to live with me. As unhappily married adults, my brother and I had speculated often about how much happier we might be, how much better we'd be at being married if we hadn't grown up in our first unhappy home.

"Let me be more specific." Angela leaned forward in her recliner. "Are you here for marriage counseling? Or divorce counseling?"

The question hung as heavily as the hammers and vice grips on the pegboard wall.

"I think we can make our marriage work," Robert said.

"I wish we could make our marriage work," I said at precisely the same moment.

Angela lived to save families, I knew. And I knew this wasn't exactly what she wanted to hear.

"Good. You both want to stay married," she said—obliviously or therapeutically, I couldn't tell. "So let's get to work. I'd like each of you to describe what's going on in your marriage. Not by blaming each other, but by owning your own part in your dynamic."

She turned to me with that look on her face, the one I'd seen her fix on Sandy Rand and her daughters—the look Hank Giarretto had fixed on me the day we met. "Meredith, I'm wondering," Angela said, "are there any issues from your childhood that might make it hard for you to trust a man?"

Again, I reached for "no." Again, "no" wouldn't come.

four

Breaking the Silence

If a man breaks into a liquor store, we say
throw the guy in jail. But if he breaks into the
body of a 4-year-old girl, we start looking for
psychological causes.

> —*Sandra Butler in Meredith Maran,*
> *"Breaking the Silence," West, May 1984*

We were both trying. Really, we were.

Robert did the laundry and took the kids to the park with
their cousins and asked before he threw my sweaters into the
washing machine.

Change the channel, I chanted when I looked at him and
felt anger, not love; when a root canal seemed preferable to the
"romance homework" Angela assigned us. *Focus on what's good.*

We couldn't make the sex dates and cuddling sessions work.
But we did do things together, family things Angela had pre-
scribed to strengthen our bond. We taught the kids to play
Hangman on our new Apple IIe. Enlisted to the cause, my brother
helped us install a bay window in our bedroom so we could sleep
with our heads in the garden. But once it was built, we pushed
our pillows to the far sides of the bed.

One morning I woke up and found Robert lying on the floor,
clutching his chest. "Call an ambulance," he gasped. "I'm having
a heart attack."

"Your heart is functioning perfectly," the ER doc said. "Are you under some kind of stress?"

On the way home, Robert and I talked more deeply, more honestly than we had in years. Neither of us was happy with the decision we reached. But we were both relieved to have made it.

Angela cried when we told her that Robert would be moving out as soon as he found a place to go.

"We're hoping it's temporary," I said, comforting her, comforting myself.

Meanwhile, the word "McMartin" had become shorthand not only for a preschool in Southern California but for the particular brand of horror that is child sexual abuse.

Time Magazine
April 2, 1984
"Brutalized"

Virginia McMartin, 76, a white-haired widow, sat in a wheelchair last week in a Los Angeles superior court, her head bowed low. McMartin, three relatives and three other women faced charges that they sodomized, fondled and raped more than 100 preschool children at a day-care center run by McMartin in Manhattan Beach, a coastal suburb of Los Angeles.

To frighten their victims into silence, the teachers allegedly cut off the ears of rabbits and other small animals in front of the children, warning the youngsters that the same fate could befall them.

"Virginia McMartin was a sweet little old lady," said an incredulous father, whose three-year-old son and seven-year-old daughter were, in his words, "brutalized" at the center. "We thought it was the best place for our children."

It broke all the therapeutic rules, but it worked somehow: seeing Angela in her garage for my marriage counseling one day, watching her struggling to glue the Rand family back together the next. I was skeptical about PU's reunification philosophy, but I couldn't help admiring Angela's commitment to the goal.

Almost a year after Jim Rand had been paroled from prison, it was time for the Rand women to decide whether he could come home. Just before the session in which that decision would be made, Angela and I sat together in the funky PU staff room.

"They've all made so much progress," Angela mused. "The five of them can be in a room together. Jim has a much better grip on what motivated the molest. Sandy's self-esteem was nearly nonexistent when we started. She can stand up to Jim now."

Angela dunked a Lipton tea bag into a chipped white mug. "And the girls." She looked up at me, smiling. "Rachel's learning to live her own life, instead of playing mother to her sisters and her mom. I'm encouraging her to go away to college next year, instead of living at home.

"I'm still concerned about the younger two, especially Lisa," Angela said. "She's so hooked into her dad. The father-daughter bond is important for a girl her age. But it has to be based on her strength, not her fear."

Angela sighed. "Oh, well. We'll get her there." She glanced at the Timex on her wrist, took a sip of tea, and pushed herself back from the table. "Decision time," she said.

I followed her downstairs. She paused outside her office and nodded at the observation room next door. "Sandy asked that you observe this session through the one-way mirror," she told me with an apologetic look.

Even through the one-way mirror, the tension between the Rands was palpable. I turned up the intercom, pen poised.

"Just for today," Angela began, "Jim will speak first."

Instead of his usual pullover, sneakers, and jeans, Jim wore a white button-down shirt, ironed khakis, and shiny black leather shoes. "Do you mind if I stand up while I talk?" he asked Angela. "It's hard to make eye contact with everyone when I'm sitting down."

"*We* sit down when *we* talk," Rachel said. "So you can sit down, too."

Jim flushed and sank into his seat. "I just want to make sure you all hear me. I'm going to speak to you from the deepest place in my heart. I think you know how sorry I am for what I did—"

"Please name it, Jim," Angela interjected.

"You know how sorry I am for the molest," he corrected himself. "I'll never do anything like that again." He fixed his eyes on Lisa. "You know how much I love you."

Sandy draped her arm around Sarah, but she didn't engulf her daughter the way she used to do.

"I've learned so much about myself in this process," Jim continued. "I know what my triggers are. I can control them. If you'll just give me the honor of taking me back, I promise to be the husband and father I should have been."

His dark eyes filled with tears. "The husband and father you deserve," he said.

"The girls and I made a decision," Sandy said in a firm voice I'd never heard her use before. "We want to leave things the way they are."

Jim's wet eyes widened. "Are you saying I can't come home?"

"It's not your home anymore," Sandy said in that same voice. "The girls and I are still learning to trust each other. We can't live with you until that happens."

"Mom," Rachel said. "Don't make it sound like he can come back. It's final. He's *out*."

Lisa started to cry. "I don't agree with them," she told her father. "I miss you. After Rachel goes away to college, I hope you come back."

"And . . ." Angela prompted her.

Lisa blew her nose. "I asked if I could live with you," she told Jim. "Just the two of us. But Angela said no."

"I said I didn't think it was a good idea. But actually, it was your mother's decision," Angela corrected her gently.

Jim's face shut like a fist. He fell back against the couch, head in hands.

"I'm sorry," Sandy murmured.

"For what?" Angela asked.

"He's my husband. I know this decision is best for my daughters. But I took a vow."

"Mom! How can you *say* that?" Rachel cried. "You're worried about your *wedding vows*, after what he did to us? He did it to you too, you know. He cheated on you. With your *daughters*."

"Stop it!" Lisa shouted. She faced Angela, feet planted, hands on her prepubescent hips. "I knew this would happen. That's why I didn't want to come. I want to go home now."

Jim lifted his head. His face was crimson.

"Go home?" Jim shouted at Lisa. "Do you know what *I'm* going home to?" He turned to Sandy. "You get to live in the house I bought and paid for with the sweat of twenty years. And where do I get to live? In a *halfway house* with a bunch of *pervs*."

Angela jumped to her feet. "That's enough, Jim," she snapped. "Don't say another word. Go to the break room and wait for me."

Jim's fists were clenched, his shoulders tensed around his ears. He took a half-step toward Angela. *He's going to hit her,* I thought.

Just try it, Angela's two-hundred-pound, unmoving body warned him. Jim stomped out of the room, slamming the door behind him.

"I *told* you he'd get mad," Lisa cried. "Nobody would *listen* to me."

Wincing with the effort, Angela lowered herself onto her knees in front of Lisa. "Sweetheart." She took Lisa's chin in her hand. "Just because your dad wants something, that doesn't mean you have to give it to him."

"But I want him," Lisa wailed. "I want my dad."

"You want a dad who can take care of you." Angela laid the palm of her hand on Lisa's cheek, crooning to her. "Of course you do. But your dad isn't ready to be that kind of father. If he was, he'd be able to put his daughters' needs ahead of his own."

Lisa's shoulders were still shaking.

"Maybe someday," Angela said. "But not now."

Angela stood and turned to the others. "Do you want to stay and process this? Or—"

Sandy pulled Sarah to her feet. She beckoned to Lisa and Rachel and she told Angela, "I'm taking my daughters home."

We were living apart, but Robert and I kept slogging through marriage—no, *divorce* counseling with Angela. She was still rooting for reconciliation, but whatever the eventual outcome, we needed an interim plan.

Neither of us could bear to live without our four- and five-year-old boys for more than a day or two. So Robert moved into a friend's spare room. On Wednesday nights and weekends, I moved out of our house and he moved in.

"Daddy and I are taking a little vacation from each other. He's going to be sleeping over at Scott's house a few nights a week," I told the boys. "And I'm going to sleep at Heidi's sometimes."

"Can we go on vacation *with* you?" Matthew asked, prompting me to worry that I was giving my kids a warped concept of vacations, not to mention marriage.

"I want to spend the night at Heidi's," Charlie chimed in.

"I'll ask Heidi if we can all sleep over next time," I said. Heidi said yes, as she always did, and the four of us—this new four of us—had a great time.

Thank goddess for Heidi. We'd known each other for a couple of years, since Robert brought Charlie to a union meeting and came home with Heidi, who'd fallen in love with Charlie and wanted to meet his brother and his mom. She and I had been through some heavy stuff already: cancer (hers), marriage troubles (mine), boyfriend ecstasies and agonies (hers), and scarily sick babies (mine). She'd helped me mother my boys in more ways than I could count.

The first few Wednesday nights and Saturday mornings, I arrived at Heidi's house in tears, collapsing into her arms before her door had quite closed behind me. Grief burned my chest, my throat, my bones. I wanted to give my kids the family my brother and I hadn't had. Instead I was giving them the same estranged parents, the same pain my parents had given us.

After the first few bone-crushing weeks, I started spending weekends with old friends in San Francisco and Berkeley. Trying not to sound as lost as I felt, I made brunch and dinner dates with the feminist therapists and authors and activists I'd met while I was working with Roselyn. Most of them were lesbians, older than I was and childless by choice.

Their world was new to me, exotic and exciting. I mimicked their in-jokes and their outfits, embarrassed by my own eagerness to join the in-club but too intrigued to stop. They took me to gay bars, and I sat sipping white russians, staring at the men slow-dancing with men and at the women cruising women, crossing and uncrossing my legs.

I'd chosen Angela to be our marriage counselor because I'd seen how fiercely she advocated for kids. Now Robert and I had to decide what would be best for ours. The options weren't good.

"Do you want to move back in together?" Angela asked. "Or do you want to talk about divorce?"

I knew what she was doing. I'd seen her do "paradoxical interventions" with the Rands, seeming to lead them toward a conclusion in order to show them that it wasn't where they wanted to go.

This time her trick backfired. Robert shot me a furious look. *You picked her,* he accused me silently. *And now look where we are.*

"Maybe we should talk about divorce," he said.

I made an appointment with a paralegal. Maybe by the time we saw her, I thought, I'd be a better person, a better wife. Maybe by then I'd be able to stop focusing on what Robert was teaching our sons with his frozen peas and his flash-fire temper, and start focusing on what a good father he was to them—so much better than my father had been to me.

On a single night in April, both the CBS Evening News and the ABC Evening News featured segments about the McMartin case. Two weeks later, Tom Brokaw reported on sexual abuse accusations against the founder of a children's theater company in Minneapolis. That same week, Peter Jennings anchored a special called *Special Assignment: Child Abuse.*

I'd been covering child sexual abuse for a while, so most new books and studies on the subject made their way to me. One was *Child Sexual Abuse: New Theory and Research*, by sociologist David Finkelhor. In it he estimated that up to 52 percent of American women and up to 9 percent of men had been sexually abused.

Finkelhor described the risk factors that made sexual offending more likely: maternal illness or absence, overcrowding, family stress, and emotional deprivation in the child. Refuting the argument that American society is based on free will and so children can choose to accept or refuse adults' sexual advances, Finkelhor pointed out that true consent is only possible if a person has knowledge and authority. Children, he observed, lacked both—a fact of which I was painfully aware, as Robert and I prepared to tell our kids that their mommy and daddy were getting a divorce.

They sat side by side on the plaid herculon couch in our living room, Matthew in his Superman pajamas, Charlie in his He-Man Underoos, their faces clean and shining, foamy drifts of bubble bath clinging to their hair.

When I said the D word Matthew exploded, his wiry body a tiny tornado of grief. He catapulted off the couch, ricocheting around the room. "No, Mommy! No! No, Daddy!" he cried. "Please! Please!"

As his brother wept and wailed, Charlie sat silently, watching. I wrapped my arms around his skinny body.

"How do *you* feel, Charlie?" I asked.

His dad knelt in front of him. "Do you know Mommy and Daddy still love you?" he implored.

Charlie would not be hurried or cajoled. As always, he composed his thoughts before he spoke. "When Daddy's not with me, Mommy will be with me," he said. "When Mommy's not with me, Daddy will be with me. I'll be okay, because someone will be with me all the time."

Robert and I stared at each other over Charlie's curly head. I tasted the tears coursing down my face. I saw the tears slickening his. *I'm not sure about that,* I didn't say to my wise, self-soothing son. *I'm not sure that any of us will be okay.*

They won't hear us fighting anymore, I told myself, driving the kids to preschool in the mornings. *They won't grow up in an unhappy household the way Doug and I did.*

Feeding them dinner at night, three of us sitting where four belonged, I was less sanguine. *Great,* I thought. *They'll grow up in an unhappy divorce instead.*

The financial problems our family faced paled in comparison to the emotional swamp we were slogging through together and separately, but they had to be solved nonetheless. Robert earned $5.25 an hour as an apprentice machinist. With my paltry freelance income, we could barely fund one household, let alone two. I called a few of Roselyn's therapist friends, looking for editing work. I got lucky: one of them hired me to edit her book about gay senior citizens.

When I'd started interviewing people about child sexual abuse, several of them had asked if there was incest in my past.

Now that I was editing a book by a lesbian shrink, people were asking if there was a woman in my future. I hadn't been able to say no to the possibility of incest then. And I couldn't say no to the possibility of a woman now.

Because, incredibly, there *was* the possibility of a woman. Jane, the woman I'd met in Dallas the year before, had been writing to me, and I'd been writing back. Our letters were light and newsy, the careful correspondence of two women becoming friends. I was married, after all, and straight.

But six weeks after Robert moved out, Jane wrote to say she was coming to San Francisco to visit an old friend. She wanted to see me. She wanted to meet my husband and my kids.

I felt the same clutch I'd felt in Dallas, that disconcerting mix of excitement and fear. I was still hoping that somehow, someday, Robert and I would get back together. How could that happen if I was *gay*?

Kids, yes, I decided; husband, no. I strapped Matthew and Charlie into their car seats and drove the family Volvo to the San Jose airport to meet Jane's plane. After an awkward moment, exchanging hugs in the loading zone, we were on our way. She reached into her backpack, pulled out two gift-wrapped packages, twisted around, and handed one to each of the boys.

"Maybe you should wait till we get home to open them," she said in her soft, sweet voice. I melted, remembering the slogan on my mother's *Settlement Cookbook*: "The Way to a Man's Heart Is Through His Stomach." Apparently the way to an ambivalent, possibly bisexual woman's heart was through her kids.

Charlie and Matthew tore the wrappings off their gifts the instant they set foot in the house. "Transformers!" they howled with delight.

"More Than Meets the Eye," Jane quoted the slogan on the packages, winking at me.

She knelt on the earth-tone shag carpet on the living room floor and showed the boys how to transform their action figures. Tanks to robots and then click! Clack! Tanks again. I watched, mesmerized, wondering what kind of transformation she had in mind for me.

The shadows shifted, sunlight fading to dusk. Jane glanced at the watch on her narrow, hairless wrist. "I've got to get going," she said.

Matthew looked at her entreatingly. "Can't you spend the night?" he asked.

My face caught fire, but Jane didn't notice. She lowered herself to five-year-old-eye height. "I'm staying at my friend's house in San Francisco," she told Matthew. "But maybe I'll spend the night with you guys another time."

"Can she, Mommy?" Charlie begged.

I felt sweat gathering at my hairline. "We'll see," I said, avoiding Jane's gaze.

Later that night Jane called and asked me to meet her for lunch in the city the next day. I said yes.

It took me hours to get dressed. Was this my first date with a woman, or lunch with a new friend? I called Harriet, one of my lesbian therapist clients, and asked her what one would wear if one were dressing for lunch with one's first woman lover. Harriet laughed, sounding delighted.

"Score one for our team," she said.

I wore a white button-down shirt and pale blue linen pants, the least feminine outfit in my closet. *In my closet.* Every phrase, every thought was suddenly a freighted double entendre. *Am I becoming a lesbian?* was a drumbeat in my head. I'd had crushes on girls in elementary school, the obligatory encounter with a fellow feminist during the Sapphic seventies. But I'd never seen my future with a woman like Jane. I'd never seen my future with a woman at all.

As we picked at carne asada burritos the size of our arms—*our arms are the same size!*—I told Jane about the Rands. I was surprised to see her eyes tearing up as I spoke. *What an empathic person she is,* I thought. It really *would* be different, being with a woman.

"I want to tell you something," she said. "Something I've never told anyone else."

"Tell me," I said.

Still, she hesitated.

"You can trust me," I said. I slid out of my side of the booth and slid in next to her. The Mexican guys behind the grill stopped flipping meat and started staring at Jane and me.

"My older brother molested me," she said, and she started to cry. I put my arm around her.

The hell with what the grill guys think. The hell with what everyone thinks. This really matters.

Jane slumped against me, her shoulders shaking.

"It's okay," I murmured. She cried harder.

"You're safe now," I said.

"It feels so *big* to tell you," she choked out.

"Thank you for telling me," I said.

I held Jane, and I felt like a compassionate, caring person. Not a bad wife who didn't love her husband anymore. Not a bad mother who was wrecking her children's home.

After lunch Jane directed me to the house where she was staying. I parked in front of a charmingly crooked Potrero Hill cottage. My car's engine ticked as it cooled, a metronome keeping time.

"Let's go away together this weekend," I blurted. "My kids will be with their dad."

Jane shot me a surprised look. "Okay," she said.

And so we did.

By the time Jane went back to Massachusetts, a seed had been planted. Something was growing between us: something irresistible, tangled, dark and deep.

Two Sundays later, the *Mercury News* landed with a thump against my front door.

West Magazine
May 20, 1984
"Breaking the Silence"

As recently as 18 years ago, experts believed that incest occurred in only one in a million American families. Now, they know better.

Research conducted by Dr. Diana E.H. Russell . . . suggests that 38 percent of female children in the United States will be sexually abused in their lifetimes; similar research by Dr. David Finkelhor of the University of New Hampshire suggests that nearly 9 percent of male children will also be abused. More than 85 percent of the victims will be molested by someone they know.

Incest occurs in all ethnic and socioeconomic groups. The number of reported cases roughly parallels the percentage of a given ethnic group in the population. . . .

The majority of reported incest cases (as distinguished from the broader category of child sexual abuse) involve a father or stepfather as perpetrator, and a daughter or stepdaughter as victim. . . .

—Meredith Maran Graham

"Meredith," Angela said, "you're quiet today. What's on your mind?"

In the beanbag chair next to me, my husband—my estranged husband, now—closed his eyes.

"I'm seeing someone," I said.

Robert opened his eyes and smiled, a twisted little grin. I was surprised to see relief on his face. "That makes two of us," he said.

The finality of our separation rocked me. Dream over. Matthew and Charlie would forever be *children from a broken home.*

"Who is she?" I asked. He named a woman I vaguely knew.

"Who is *he?*" Robert asked.

I swallowed hard, staring at the delicate gold cross that dangled on Angela's neck.

"She," I said.

Silence.

"You mean—" Angela said.

"A *woman?*" Robert said at the same time.

"Yes," I said. "A woman."

My husband and my Italian Catholic therapist stared at me, mouths agape.

"Her name is Jane," I said.

Time Magazine
September 3, 1984
"Make Room for Baby"

Good professional supervision for children is often hard to find, and the possibility of child abuse is a growing concern. Working parents horrified by a series of sex scandals in day care centers around the country ... prefer company-run programs close to the office, where mothers and fathers can drop by during the day.

—*Stephen Koepp, Joyce Leviton, and Thomas McCarroll*

The next time I met with my client Harriet, she asked me, giggling, if I was out of the closet yet.

I told her about coming out to my husband. Her laughter stopped on a dime. She gave me the name and number of a lesbian lawyer.

"Call her," Harriet said.

"Why would I need a lawyer?" I asked.

"Don't make me spell it out for you."

The lawyer told me that a woman negotiating the custody of her young children would be well advised not to disclose her interest in another woman until those negotiations are resolved.

"Robert and I met on a *picket line*," I protested. "He wouldn't—"

"If he takes you to court, you should petition for a change of venue," she interrupted me. "I don't want to scare you. But unless your case is heard in a progressive jurisdiction, you could lose custody of your kids."

Scared? I was terrified. I'd die without my kids. And if there was one thing the past year had taught me, it was this. No woman ever really knew what her husband might do.

I called an emergency session with Robert and Angela. I told Robert that I wanted to work out a joint custody arrangement. To my relief, he agreed. I asked if he'd consider moving back to Oakland, where we'd met and been married, where we had friends, where my work was. I said I wanted the kids to grow up with all kinds of people, not in the all-white suburbs of San Jose.

Angela's magic didn't fail us. By the end of the session, Robert and I had agreed that I'd look for a house in Oakland, and he'd move nearby as soon as he could. In the interim, he'd see the kids in Oakland on Wednesday nights, and I'd bring them to San Jose two weekends out of three.

The next morning, I awoke from a strange dream. I scribbled it into the journal I kept beside my bed.

Journal entry, September 12, 1984

My dream:

I'm running through Central Park, knowing that it's against the law to run in Central Park unless you were molested as a child.

I'm running along toward the sailboat pond, thinking, if I get stopped I'll say I was molested as a child. I scold myself: how low that is. Then I realize that it's TRUE.

What happened when I was a child, I wondered. Was I just trying to catch Jane's disease? Or was the dream true of me?

Big news broke in the McMartin case. The investigators had found that three hundred McMartin students, past and present, had been abused by their teachers—forced to participate in orgies and to play a game called "Naked Movie Star," in which they were photographed in the nude. All of this had happened in secret underground tunnels beneath the school.

On the other side of the country, a little girl came home from the U.S. Army's child-care center in West Point, New York, bleeding from her vagina. Her classmates said their teachers had forced them to witness animal sacrifices, watch pornography, and participate in rituals with adults wearing masks.

It was happening everywhere. Three employees of the Small World preschool in Niles, Michigan, went to jail for sexually abusing their students. Miami preschool operator Frank Fuster and his seventeen-year-old wife were indicted for forcing their students to drink urine and eat feces. Florida state attorney general Janet Reno prosecuted the case.

In Pittsfield, Massachusetts, a nineteen-year-old preschool aide named Bernard Baran was charged with sexually assaulting two three-year-olds in his care. In Richmond, Virginia, a seven-year-old and a five-year-old were removed from their home after telling police that their mother and her boyfriend had sexually abused them. The children said their parents had forced them to witness the cult-ritual murder of a twelve-year-old girl. The girl's corpse was found nearby.

On the CBS Evening News, Dan Rather reported on a case in Jordan, Minnesota, in which dozens of parents were being accused of molesting their children. As Rather spoke, his forehead was furrowed, his upper lip curled, as if the words were too distasteful to speak.

I'd had doubts when I first heard the gruesome details about the McMartin case. Underground tunnels? Pedophiliac orgies? Even with my above-average awareness of adults' ability to hurt the children who trusted them most, I'd found it all nearly unimaginable.

But my doubts were being obliterated by the magnitude and the consistency of the children's reports. If those things hadn't happened to toddlers in West Point and Manhattan Beach and Jordan, how could so many kids have come up with the same horrific stories at the same time?

I brought my journal to my individual therapy with Angela and read her my latest incest dreams. When I finished she was perched on the edge of her seat, regarding me with the business end of her eyes.

"What do you make of those dreams?" she asked.

"I think I'm reading too many headlines. Watching too much TV."

Angela's gaze bored into me.

"Maybe I'm overidentifying with the kids I'm writing about," I added. "Or maybe it's my codependence with Jane."

Angela was still staring.

"What?" I asked, wanting to know what she was thinking, knowing what she was thinking, not wanting to know.

"There could be an entirely different explanation," Angela said.

Jane decided to leave the East Coast and rent an apartment in Oakland. It went without saying that we wouldn't live together. My kids weren't ready for it, I wasn't ready for it, Jane wasn't ready for it. Our relationship definitely wasn't ready for it.

Her announcement stirred my usual response to anything Jane-related: I was thrilled and stunned and terrified.

This is really happening, I thought. I'd been saying that to myself a lot. I really was moving to a new city. I really was getting divorced. I really was raising my kids in a broken home. I really was a single mother. I really was in love with a woman.

As I was walking Matthew and Charlie home from *their* session at Angela's, I asked, "Would you guys like to see Jane again sometime?"

They exchanged a glance. "Jane's nice," Matthew said, watching me, measuring my reaction. "She's fun, like a kid."

"She gave us Transformers," Charlie added. He was looking at me too, trying to figure out if that was the right answer.

They stopped walking and turned their shining, anxious faces to me. I saw that they were doing for me what the Rand girls had done for their dad, taking care of my feelings at the expense of their own.

I took Charlie's hand with my right hand and Matthew's with my left. "Just because I like Jane," I said, "doesn't mean you have to."

I felt them both relax, Charlie leaning into my right side, Matthew slumping against my left. "We *know* that, Mommy," Matthew said. He and Charlie let go of my hands and skipped ahead of me. Heart in throat, I followed them home.

I found a cozy cottage in North Oakland, three blocks from a highly rated, highly diverse public school. My mother loaned me half of the $20,000 down payment. My ex-husband bought me out of our San Jose house to cover the other half.

The day we moved in, I got an assignment from *New Age Journal.* The story was supposed to answer the question at the heart of the conflict that was raging between feminists like Roselyn Taylor and family reunification proponents like Hank Giarretto: Can incest perpetrators be rehabilitated?

The title was the top question on my kids' minds as we settled into our new, three-legged life: "Can Daddy Come Home Again?"

As I began researching the story, preliminary hearings began in the McMartin trial. The coauthors of the satanic ritual abuse memoir, *Michelle Remembers*, met with the parents of the abused McMartin kids to help them understand what their children had been through.

In Los Angeles County, police were investigating abuse allegations in sixty-three other day-care centers. *Sixty-three.*

Journal entry, November 16, 1984

My dream:

We're sitting in a movie theater and my father leans over to kiss me lightly on the lips and I am suddenly filled with an incredibly hollow empty feeling of loneliness so strong it consumes me.

In Memphis, a middle-aged teacher's aide, a Baptist minister, and two other employees of the Georgian Hills Early Childhood Center were charged with sexually assaulting and ritually abusing nineteen of their students.

In Kern County, California, two married couples were found guilty of running a sex ring and sexually abusing their own children. Each of the four was sentenced to 168 to 240 years, the longest terms ever imposed by the state of California. "You've stolen from your children the most precious of gifts," the judge told the convicted abusers, "a child's innocence."

And in Manhattan Beach, the prosecutor in the McMartin case added 397 charges of sexual abuse to the 115 charges that seven of the school's teachers already faced. Fifty McMartin parents showed up at a lot next to the school, shovels in hand. They started digging, trying to find the secret underground tunnels in which their children had been sexually abused. They found nothing, but their dig provoked the district attorney to authorize an archaeological inspection by Scientific Resource Surveys Inc. SRS didn't find anything either.

A few days later, the McMartin parent who'd made the original accusation against Ray Buckey was diagnosed and hospitalized with acute paranoid schizophrenia. I tried to imagine how I'd feel if a teacher had done to Matthew or Charlie what Ray Buckey had done to her son. *I'd probably have a breakdown, too*, I thought.

When the winter break ended, Matthew started the second half of his kindergarten year at his new school. The school in San Jose had called it "Christmas vacation." In Oakland they called it "Christmas/Hanukkah/Kwanzaa/Solstice."

After months of research and reference checks and sneak visits that put my investigative skills to their most stringent test yet, each morning I pulled Charlie close to me and then left him, God help me, at the local day-care center.

five

Daddy Can't Come Home Again

A new *Los Angeles Times* poll . . . has found that
27% of women and 16% of men were sexually
abused. . . . Applied to the current population, this
means that nearly 38 million American adults
were sexually abused as children.
—*Connie Chung, NBC Evening News,*
August 24, 1985

On assignment for "Can Daddy Come Home Again?" I flew to
Seattle, home of two pioneering incest treatment programs.

The Harborview Sexual Assault Center, founded by feminist
social worker Lucy Berliner, treated adult and child victims, most
of them female. Northwest Treatment Associates, its "brother"
program, treated perpetrators, most of them male.

Harborview and Northwest were founded in the early 1970s,
soon after Hank Giarretto founded Parents United, but not with
the goal of reintegrating perpetrators into their families.

After observing a wrenching therapy session with a nine-
year-old girl whose father had been molesting her since she
was five, I met with Lucy Berliner. Without naming PU,
Berliner told me that "many therapists" treat offenders too
sympathetically.

"Perpetrators put up a good front," she said. "They seem so
normal. But they've gotten so good at denial that they can easily

lie to anyone. Offenders are far more dangerous as a group than we've been willing to acknowledge."

Berliner added, "A family doesn't need an offender in it to be a family. We urge biological parents to work on their communication because those two people have a lifelong relationship to that child. But we also point out to mothers that agreeing to live with a sex offender means agreeing to be a supervisor for the rest of your life in order to protect the children in your home."

After what had been passing for lunch lately—I'd lost my appetite since I'd started reporting incest stories—I took a cab across town to Northwest Treatment Associates, where I was ushered into the crowded, tidy office of codirector Steven Wolf.

"Unlike Parents United," Wolf told me, "we see no difference between incestuous fathers and other child molesters. They're pedophiles, period."

As a feminist, I agreed. As a journalist, it was my job to play devil's advocate. "PU claims that less than one percent of their graduates reoffend," I said.

"That's hard to believe." Wolf frowned. "We've treated four thousand offenders here. And I can tell you that these men are incurably addicted to their sexual behavior. We treat them with the goal of controlling, not curing them."

He glanced at the clock on the wall, and then at me. "That session you wanted to observe starts in ten minutes. You sure you're up for it? It won't be pretty."

"Yes," I said, and I was. I was getting used to this.

And I *was* fine when the therapist asked whether Tim preferred sex with a woman or sex with a little girl, and Tim gave the answer that had landed him in jail two years ago. I was a little bit less fine when Tim explained why he preferred his daughter's body to his wife's: "Silky skin, slender arms, soft all over."

But then the therapist took a child-size, anatomically correct, blonde-haired, blue-eyed blow-up doll out of the closet, handed it to Tim, and told him to reenact the crimes he'd inflicted on his three-year-old child. I watched, taking notes, as long as I could. Longer than I could. And then I turned my eyes away.

When the session finally ended, I rushed out of the clinic and into the first phone booth I saw. I called Heidi, who was staying with my kids, and asked her to put them on the phone.

"Only one more day, Mommy," said seven-year-old Matthew, family statistician, keeper of the maternal absence countdown.

"Heidi made hot dogs for dinner," Charlie reported. He lowered his voice to a stage whisper. "But they were gross."

I confirmed Matthew's calculations, reassured Charlie that the tofu dogs were a temporary indignity, and sent them cartoon kisses through the phone.

When I tried to sleep I saw Tim. Tim with his hands all over the party doll. Tim with his hands all over his daughter. I felt like throwing up and I felt like crying and I felt like calling my therapist.

My *therapist.* The thought of Angela usually calmed me down. Not tonight. Angela worked at Parents United. She believed what Parents United said, that girls like Sara, Lisa, and Rachel could be safe in their homes with their rapist fathers in the bedroom next door. I'd watched her trying to work that miracle, trying to believe it. But I didn't. I didn't.

Could Daddy come home again?

No, he couldn't. If watching Jim Rand's therapy sessions hadn't convinced me of that, watching Tim's had.

As hard as I'd been trying to be the objective journalist—to explore with equal curiosity the possibility that incest perpetrators could be cured and the possibility that they could never be—the truth was, I would never have allowed Jim Rand or Tim anywhere near a child I loved.

I remembered what a feminist therapist had told me in an interview a couple of years before, when I'd asked if she worried that innocent men would get swept up in the campaign to imprison molesters. "If one innocent man goes to prison in the course of stopping a hundred abusers," she'd told me, "that's a price we should be willing to pay."

Her answer had shocked me then, but it made perfect sense to me now.

Letter to Jane, August 1, 1985

I woke up this morning from intense dreams. I had told someone the truth about what really happened to me as a child. What had really happened was that I had been raped, very young.

The memory had broken through my occlusion like the sun through clouds and I was at peace at last. And I woke up knowing with great certainty that something DID happen to me as a child. And I doubt myself and think I'm being melodramatic and yet these dreams keep repeating that it's true. And I keep writing incest articles.

Jane and I continued as we had begun: intensely.

We connected intensely. We made love intensely. We made puns and laughed intensely, we talked about the things that mattered to us intensely, and we fought about big stuff and stupid stuff with the kind of intensity that left no nerve ending unsinged.

And so, although our relationship felt like a miracle to me— what were the odds I'd meet a lesbian who gave me the passion and intimacy I'd ached for in my marriage, a woman who loved my children as intensely as she loved me—Jane and I saw a lesbian-affirmative couple's counselor once a week.

"The issue between you two isn't power," the therapist said, looking from one of us to the other. "It's trust."

"I'm an incest survivor," Jane said.

The therapist nodded, as if that explained everything, which I supposed it did. My turn. What to say?

"I had an unhappy childhood," I said.

I don't even have a good excuse, I thought.

The New York Times
January 27, 1985
"Boy's Responses at Sex Abuse Trial
Underscore Legal Conflict"

He is a small, sandy-haired child named Willie. Matter-of-factly, he answers yes, he was sexually molested by his teachers at the Virginia McMartin Pre-School. . . . [Defense attorney] Mr. Latiner asserted "every psychological expert will tell you children fantasize about sex," including, he maintained, fantasies about sex involving adults.

—Robert Lindsay

I decided to stop seeing Angela. The reasons to continue had finally been outnumbered by the reasons to quit: the hour-long commute from Oakland to San Jose. My shaky, single-mother finances. My immersion in a lesbian world that was alien to Angela despite her best intentions. And most of all, my inability to reconcile my trust in her with my growing distrust of the Parents United philosophy.

Angela greeted my news with an offer to reduce her fee. When I gratefully declined, she pulled me to her in a grandmotherly embrace.

"We'll still see each other when you're researching your stories," she said, wiping her wet eyes. My own eyes stinging, I said, "Of course we will." But I knew we wouldn't.

How could I protect Matthew and Charlie from the awful things that had happened to Jane when she was their age, the awful things that were happening to children everywhere every day?

I brought cupcakes to Charlie's kindergarten class and found myself scrutinizing his classmates, looking for signs. I accompanied Matthew's first-grade class on a field trip to Oakland Children's Hospital, wondering which of them might end up there because some adult had done to them what the worst kind of adults do to kids.

In November 1985, I settled onto my king-size bed with my sons to watch an ABC after-school movie called *Don't Touch*.

"What's *molested?*" Matthew asked when the first commercial rolled. Charlie studied my face.

"It's when an adult hurts a child," I answered, "by touching his or her private parts."

Matthew and Charlie looked at each other, and I swear I heard their silent exchange. "It's okay for you to touch yourself," I reassured them. "You don't hurt yourself when you do that."

The movie resumed. Karen, the teenage protagonist, remembered having been molested by her uncle when she was very young. This compelled her to tell Molly's parents that Molly, too, was being sexually abused.

"Karen's brave, like MacGyver," Charlie observed. "She saved Molly."

Charlie saw Karen saving Molly. I saw myself saving Jane. Or was it myself I was saving?

Our family was celebrating Matthew's seventh birthday in our backyard with twenty of his closest friends.

The Pac-Man piñata swung from the apple tree, the picnic table was piled high with brightly wrapped presents, the homemade poppy-seed cake was candled-up and ready to go. It was early December, the season of rain for northern California. But the winter sky shone on my sunshine boy.

Robert was prepping the partygoers for their turns at bat: blindfolding each boy, then spinning him around and giving him a gentle shove toward Jane. Jane handed each batter the broomstick that would, eventually, do the job. Heidi was photo-documenting, cheering from behind the lens.

I loved these three people the way only one parent can love another: from the parental gut. Gazing at this Rockwellesque scene, this maybe-not-so-broken family, I thought: *Is this good life my life? My children's lives?* My remorseful heart flickered with faint hope. *Maybe they're having a happy childhood after all.*

I went into the house in search of matches and saw that the mail had dropped through the slot in the door. Among the bills and Sierra Club solicitations, a thick brown legal-size envelope. I pulled out the sheaf of documents it contained. The grin faded from my face.

I'd known the final divorce decree would be coming soon. But did it have to arrive today?

The New York Times
December 15, 1985
"Sex-Case Defense Assails Therapists"

For nearly two months, in a nearly deserted courtroom, the teachers and administrators accused of sexually abusing scores of children at a pre-school in nearby Manhattan Beach have presented an unusual defense....

The defendants' attorneys say that the charges of sexual abuse . . . were based not on fact but on fantasy. They argue that the fantasy was created in response to suggestive questions posed first by apprehensive parents and then by therapists who were asked by prosecutors to interview the children to try to determine if they had been molested.

—Marcia Chambers

Journal entry, December 24, 1985

My dream:

I'm on my bed with a woman, telling her about my father. "The problem is, when I see him I never know if we're still being sexual or if it's stopped." As I'm saying this I have a vision of my father's hand—his knuckles—like a fist. "All my life I've never known when it would stop: the sexual dynamic. I've been waiting for him to stop it, since the feeling is that it's my fault."

Lucky me: Heidi fell in love with a guy who lived in Oakland. She moved to a small house a few blocks from ours to be close to him, and to the kids and me.

The few fights I'd had with Heidi in the six years we'd been best friends had all adhered to the Jew-Gentile script. Heidi's constitutional optimism seemed to me proof of chronic denial. My perennial pessimism brought her down. But lately we'd been sharing an experience that transcended the Easter-versus-Passover polarity. Heidi was having incest dreams, too.

"Do you actually think your father . . . ?" I asked.

"Dad would never do that to me," she said.

"Then what do you think your dreams are about?" I asked.

Since we'd met, Heidi had been trying to recruit me to Re-evaluation Counseling, a layperson's therapy group with roots in the anti-psychiatry, pro-social-change movement of the 1970s. After completing a course in basic counseling techniques, co-counselors traded sessions, exchanging attention and time instead of money.

I'd been missing the sanctuary of my sessions with Angela, and the freebie aspect of co-counseling appealed to me. But the group was eerily cultish, with rigid party lines about everything, it seemed. Of course, that didn't stop me from poaching a psychological insight or two from my co-counseling friend.

"I think my incest dreams are a metaphor," she said.

"For what?"

"For my powerlessness as a daughter."

I considered this. "I wasn't powerless as a daughter. I fought with my father all the time."

Heidi regarded me skeptically. "Fighting doesn't mean you have power," she said. "It means you don't."

"I hate it when you're right," I conceded.

The movie version of *The Color Purple*, Alice Walker's much-censored portrayal of incest in the 1930s American South, was nominated for a record-breaking eleven Academy Awards.

Defending the brutal story at the heart of her novel, Walker said, "This is the country in which a woman is raped every three minutes, where one out of three women will be raped during their lifetimes. And a quarter of those are children under twelve."

The New York Times
March 19, 1986
"Child Sex Abuse Said to Rise"

Reports of sexual abuse of children increased 59 percent from 1983 to 1984, and most of the children were abused at home by parents, a recent study has reported. . . .

[An expert said that] studies had "left the public thinking that child abuse is leveling off or even decreasing and that the majority of the reports are unsubstantiated." He added, "This is not true."

—*UPI*

My father called to tell me he was retiring and moving to San Francisco with his third wife, a woman six years older than

I was, a woman eighteen years younger than my dad. "We want to get to know the grandkids," he said.

My body clenched. I was used to dealing with my father in my head, to say the least. But I wasn't used to dealing with him in the flesh. My father and I hadn't lived on the same continent since I'd left home at age seventeen. Now he and his new wife were going to live just one short bridge away from my kids and me.

"Great," I said through gritted teeth.

"Better late than never," my brother said sarcastically when we talked about our father's news. My brother's kids were six and eight; mine were six and seven. Our father was the only grandfather they had.

As my father's arrival neared, my senseless heart started sending up flares of hope. Maybe having my father in my life again would bring us closer, the way we'd been when I was a kid. Maybe seeing him as an actual human being instead of a lurking ghost would quash my nightmares and fears.

Sure enough, my first thought when I saw my father was, *He couldn't have.*

My father wasn't Jim Rand, or Tim the daughter-rapist, or even Jane's lecherous big brother. He was *my dad*, in all his funny, distracted, disappointing glory. My dad, the former executive who said, "I'm just glad I retired before they caught on to how incompetent I am."

Over the next few months my brother and I tried our kids' new grandfather on for size. Gloria was an enthusiastic if inexperienced grandparent, but my father talked to his young grandkids the way he'd talked to my brother and me: as if they were miniature adults. Just as he'd done with us, he lost interest by the time they got two sentences into their bubbly, babbly stories.

With Gloria leading the way, my father and Gloria showed Matthew, Charlie, Emmy, and Zach a great time, taking them to play miniature golf, to children's museums, to Chinatown dim sum brunch. I convinced myself that my dreams were just dreams, my suspicions misguided empathy.

"How can you leave your kids with him?" Jane asked me. "And what about Emmy? Don't you think you should tell your brother?"

"Tell my brother what?" I said. "I still don't know what happened."

"You have to believe yourself," Jane said. "Feelings don't lie. Dreams don't lie."

I didn't tell my brother, and I didn't stop leaving my kids with my dad. I didn't want to deprive them of their only grandfather, the adventures with their cousins, the middle-class benefits package my father had offered me. So I watched my father warily as he tossed the boys into the air and caught them. I winced when he pulled Emmy onto his lap. I gave my kids baths after days they spent with him, inspecting their bodies surreptitiously.

My head was a jangling kaleidoscope of loose, shifting truths. My dad, the loving grandfather. My father, the child molester. Me, the good daughter and good mother. Me, the crazy paranoiac. Too many versions of reality added up to none.

One Sunday evening, I was driving Matthew and Charlie home from a sleepover at Grandpa and Granny's, and I glanced in the rearview mirror and saw Charlie looking worried. I asked if he was okay.

"Grandpa got mad at Charlie and threw him down on the couch really hard," Matthew piped up. "Charlie cried."

Charlie looked embarrassed and relieved. "I couldn't help it," he said. "Grandpa was mean."

I literally saw red. I pulled the car over, took several breaths, and turned to face my boys. "Is Grandpa gonna get in trouble?" Matthew asked, looking scared.

I remembered Sarah Rand, protecting her abusive father. "Any grownup who hurts a child deserves to be in trouble," I said.

"It was a *couch*, Mommy," Charlie said. "He didn't throw me on the floor. It didn't even hurt."

I remembered my father slapping me in the face as a child, as a teenager. I remembered the time, shortly before I left home for good, when I'd slapped him back.

As soon as the kids were asleep, I called my father.

"You know how kids exaggerate," he said.

Where had I heard that before? Oh yes: from the child molesters and incestuous fathers and ritual abusers I'd been interviewing and reading about for the past few years.

"My kids don't exaggerate," I said. "My kids don't lie."

"All kids lie. You lied."

I lied to get out from under you.

"You're making a big deal out of nothing," my father added, his voice rising. "As usual."

I felt the sting of his slap on my face. I wanted to slap him back. I wanted to slap him back, and I wanted to stop feeling the way he was making me feel, and I wanted to get out from under him so I'd never feel this way again.

"I don't—I'm not—" My voice was broken. My father had broken it. Again. I hung up the phone.

The next time Gloria called to invite the kids over to their apartment, I told her that from then on, I was going to stay with the kids while they spent time with her and my father. She didn't ask why. I didn't tell.

Months after I'd researched and written it, my story for *New Age Journal*—the hardest piece I'd ever worked on—finally appeared.

In June, the book I'd edited for Roselyn Taylor was published to great acclaim. *The Incest Secret* earned rave reviews and several prestigious awards.

What a difference a half-decade had made. When I was editing Roselyn's book, the culture had been in a persistent vegetative state where incest was concerned. The feminists' findings, once considered scandalous, were ubiquitous now.

New Age Journal
May 1986
"The Incest Controversy:
Can Daddy Come Home Again?"

...At Seattle's Sexual Assault Center, Lucy Berliner sees victims as young as three years old. The impact of chronic sexual abuse on a child, Berliner believes, is similar to a soldier's wartime experience—with one major difference. "Like soldiers, molested kids develop defenses to help them survive ongoing trauma. But unlike a nineteen-year-old GI, these kids are still becoming who they are. So their coping responses may actually become integrated into their personalities: the way they think, the way they look at the world."

"Victims can't recover," Berliner says, "until they've had a chance to respond as normal, healthy kids would—with rage, grief, loss."

—Meredith Maran

I allowed myself a moment of pride for my part in breaking the story. If media coverage was any indicator—and it was, of course—America's best kept family secret was no secret anymore.

Jane's memories, Jane's nightmares, Jane's issues were so much more real than my shadowy suspicions. I was relieved to cede the attention to her, to let my own incest work subside, to focus on hers instead.

When we spent the night together and she woke up screaming, when she startled at the ring of the phone or a knock at the door or the sight of her own shadow, I was her champion, her protector. As I went about my business, pitching my incest queries and doing my incest interviews and writing my incest articles, she was my damsel to avenge.

When therapists and experts and survivors asked about my connection to the issue, I had a ready answer—an answer that turned the mirror away from me. When I sat in sessions with apologetic and defiant pedophiles and weeping wives and traumatized children, I didn't have to wonder why I was there. I was there to save Jane and all the little girls like her. I was there to keep what happened to her from happening to anyone ever again.

The Los Angeles Times
October 9, 1986
"Couple File $2-Million Suit Over Sex Charges"

A Massachusetts couple arrested last summer on a crowded San Clemente beach for kissing their toddler's rump filed a $2-million federal lawsuit Wednesday against the city and Police Chief Kelson McDaniel.

San Clemente police arrested the DiAngelises after a witness said she saw them molesting their 13-month-old son. . . .

In a June 30 interview, McDaniel said he believed that the parents were guilty of "deviant behavior" because they kissed their child on "an orifice." However, he said the Police Department lacked enough evidence to prosecute the couple.

—Jane Applegate

Jane and I went out to dinner at our favorite Chinese dive with another lesbian couple. Jessie was a student in the women's writing class I taught. Her girlfriend, Cathy, was what we called a "T.I.T." Like half the women I knew, it seemed, she was a therapist in training.

Over hot-and-sour soup, the conversation turned to incest, as conversations had a tendency to do. Since I'd moved to

Oakland I'd been living in a mostly women's world, teaching an all-women writing class, buying holiday gifts at wimmin's crafts fairs and books at wimmin's bookstores, dancing at wimmin's bars, listening to wimmin's music, seeing women therapists, and going to women's support groups.

The lesbian therapists whose books I was editing told me that more and more of their clients were trying to uncover memories of childhood sexual abuse, wanting to be hypnotized, wanting help writing letters to their fathers and planning confrontations with their moms.

"I have an idea for a book," Jessie said. Inwardly I groaned. Incest was the chosen topic of most of the women I taught, including Jessie. If I'd had a thousand dollars for every student who was writing an unpublishable incest memoir, I would have been in Donald Trump's tax bracket.

"We're going to write it together," Cathy chimed in. "It'll be Jessie's experience of being an incest survivor, juxtaposed with my story as the partner of a survivor."

"Tell us what you think of the title." Jessie spooned kung pao shrimp onto her plate, pausing theatrically. "*Incest in Two Voices*," she intoned.

Jane put her fork down. "There's got to be a market for that," she said. "Partners need support, too."

I shot Jane a surprised look. The jousting match between her need for support and mine had paid for quite a few therapists' *New Yorker* subscriptions in the past few years. It was worth it, though: the war we were fighting wasn't just between the two of us. Our issues were epic; the stakes were sky high. We were fighting every power struggle in history—*herstory*. In our battle, the spoils went to the victim. The crown went to the Queen of Pain.

Jane was the winner of the victim jackpot. She was an incest survivor, not an incest *suspector* like me. In her individual therapy, she was starting to recover memories of her father molesting her. Her father had died when she was only five years old.

All I had was my ever-shifting suspicions and my growing feeling of abandonment. No wonder our relationship required constant professional care.

"*Incest in Two Voices*," I repeated. "That's a great idea."

Brides Magazine
December 1986
"When a Sexually Abused Child Weds"

"Making the commitment to marriage brings up all of the issues connected with the betrayal of being molested: intimacy, trust, sexuality," says Padma Moyer, MFCC, a San Francisco, California therapist who works with adult survivors of incest.

"And when marriage is perceived as an obligation to take care of their partners' sexual needs, it recapitulates their worst childhood experience—being trapped and unable to say no."

... Dr. Judith Herman found that 65% of adult incest survivors suffered from severe depression, 55% had sexual problems, and 45% became alcoholics or drug addicts. ... Selective amnesia is common among survivors, whose memories may be blocked by years of threats to "keep Daddy's secret—or else," and by the tendency of the childhood psyche to repress traumatic experiences.

—*Meredith Maran*

six

Remember

So far, no one we've talked to thought she might
have been abused, and then later discovered
that she hadn't been. . . . If you think you were
abused and your life shows the symptoms, then
you were.

—*Ellen Bass and Laura Davis,*
The Courage to Heal, *1988*

One night in December of 1987 my bedside phone rang, late.
I grabbed it before it woke the kids.

"Hello, Meredith," my father said in that I'm-in-charge-here
voice of his, the voice that had made my pulse race and my heart
pound with anticipation and fear for as long as I could remember.
I sat up in bed, rearranging pillows behind my head.

"I'm calling to invite your family to Christmas dinner,"
my father said.

"*Christmas?*" I said, reflexively reverting to our shared language, New York Jewish sarcasm. "What—did you convert?"

"They're no fools, those goyim," my father snapped right
back. "Why buy eight nights of presents when you can get away
with one?"

That was my dad. Matching my wisecracks tit for tat.

Tit for tat? My mind started spinning, chasing that rabbit
around the track.

Isn't hypersexualizing a symptom? A sign? I made a mental note to ask my therapist when I saw her next.

How long till I see her? Uh-oh. Not for two whole days.

I reached for my bedside mug of Calming Tea. What if my father sensed the terrible things I'd been thinking and dreaming and saying about him to my lover, my friends, my shrink?

He'd always had a freakish knack for crawling inside my head whenever he felt like it—that is, when he wasn't a million metaphorical or geographical miles away. When my dad was paying attention, he seemed to know what I was thinking before I did, and he seemed to be paying attention now. I was thirty-five years old, for goddess's sake, and still that voice of my father's was a snake charmer's flute, making me sway unsteadily.

"Are Doug and Susie and the kids coming?" I stalled. Until I knew the truth, I'd decided, I'd only spend time with him and expose my sons to him in the presence of my brother and his wife and kids.

"Doug who?" my father teased, intimate now, flirtatious. His joke might have been funny if it weren't so true—if he hadn't attached himself to me when I was a kid, as if he didn't have a son. As if I didn't have a mother or a brother. As if it were just the two of us.

"Of course Doug will be there," my father said in that impatient voice of his. My pulse ticked up a notch, reading the early warning signs. It was always hard to know which father I was dealing with: warm, funny, insightful Good Daddy, or self-centered, judgmental Bad Dad. It could be dangerous, mistaking one for the other.

"We'd love to come," I said. "What can we bring?"

My father fell silent. What had I done to piss him off now?

"*We?*" he said finally. "Just to clarify, Meredith: this is a family event. So of course that doesn't include Jane."

"Are you kidding?" I said. "Jane's my—my . . ."

My *lover?* I couldn't say the word. "Jane's been raising your grandsons for the past three years."

"You're in a homosexual relationship, Meredith. You could be with Jane for the next twenty years, and your relationship still wouldn't be legitimate."

Before I could speak, my father pulled his old trick, bringing in the big guns.

"It's not legitimate in my eyes," he repeated, "or in the eyes of the law."

I set my mug down on the nightstand, took a deep breath, silently chanting the mantra my therapist had given me. *I'm a grown-up now. He can't hurt me anymore.*

Oh, but he could. I was a helpless child, fighting tears, losing.

"I thought you *liked* Jane," I croaked.

Beginning with my first boyfriend and ending with the husband I'd divorced four years ago, my father had ignored, mocked, or scorned everyone I'd loved—until Jane. I'd told myself he found a female lover less threatening. What an idiot I'd been.

"I'm sure Jane's a perfectly decent person," my father said, "but she'll never be a member of our family."

No wonder this felt so familiar. My father was doing what he'd always done. Punishing me for loving someone else. Claiming me and rejecting me. Forcing me to choose between pleasing him and being who I was.

"Matthew and Charlie love her," I said. I heard myself pleading and hated the sound of it and couldn't seem to stop. "I love her. Doesn't that matter to you at all?"

"I can see how damaged your children are," my father said.

Damaged? My beautiful boys?

"Matthew and Charlie are clearly disturbed by your homosexuality," he added.

My life with my father flashed before me. The childhood years of wanting and worshipping him. The adolescent years of battling him. The adult years of missing him, blaming him, longing for him. And the past few years, suspecting him.

Now I knew the truth. Good Daddy was a front. He didn't care about who I was or what I needed. He only cared about how I made him feel. Of *course* he was capable of using me for his own pleasure, discarding me when he was through. He was doing it now.

My incest nightmares weren't fantasies. They were memories. *My father's big, blunt hands. The wiry black hairs on his knuckles. The white half-moons of his fingernails, perfectly trimmed, perfectly clean. The scream in my throat no no no no no . . .*

"You're wrong about my kids," I said. "You're wrong about me."

"You never could stand to hear the truth about yourself," my father said. "That's why you surround yourself with weak-minded people who don't question you. I'm the only one who knows the real you."

I kicked the covers off my legs. "I want you *out of me* once and for all," I shouted.

My father started sputtering. Admitting, denying, it didn't matter anymore.

"I *do* know the truth about myself," I said. "And I know the truth about you. Don't ever call me again," I slammed down the phone.

My bedroom door flew open. Nine-year-old Matthew stood in the doorway, blonde curls tousled, hazel eyes glittering with fear. "Why are you yelling, Mommy?" he asked. He crawled into bed with me, wrapped his skinny arms around my neck. "What's wrong?"

With Matthew's puppy-smell in my nose, his moist, trusting hands on my face, I zoomed back to my real life, my real family, safe and sweet. "It's okay, honey," I whispered. "I won't yell anymore."

I don't need my father's truth anymore. I have my own now.

I gathered my limp, sleepy son into my arms and carried him back to his bed.

> ## *The New York Times*
> ### September 13, 1987
> ### "Preschool Founder Is Warned in Abuse Trial"
>
> A judge has threatened to imprison [Virginia McMartin], the 80-year-old founder of a Manhattan Beach preschool in a trial on child molestation charges after she shouted, accused the prosecutor of lying and demanded that the judge treat her with respect.
>
> [Prosecutor] Rubin asked a series of questions, once saying, "In fact, Mrs. McMartin, you knew Raymond Buckey had a problem with touching the genitals of children, didn't you?"
>
> "No, I didn't!" Mrs. McMartin shouted. "Don't try to put words in my mouth!" As the prosecutor tried to continue her inquiry, Mrs. McMartin shouted, "You're lying!"
>
> —AP

At precisely 4 P.M., Dr. Brill appeared in the waiting room doorway and led me into her office, a fluorescent cage of right angles, polyester upholstery, and plastic walnut veneer.

I'd found her name on the "Psychiatrist" list provided by my health insurer. None of the A names sounded good to me, and I hadn't had the wherewithal to get to the Cs.

"What brings you here?" Dr. Brill asked with no apparent interest.

"I need something to help me sleep."

Dr. Brill frowned. Clearly I'd violated protocol. But I was too exhausted to pretend I was there for anything else. "You'll have to tell me more than that," she said.

If I wanted my pills, I had to play along. But how to tell her what she was pretending to want to know?

I hadn't spoken to my father since our phone-fight a month ago, and my incest dreams had given way to relentless insomnia.

I'd lost my appetite for food, sex, life. I'd been delivering my kids to school in the mornings, then crawling back into bed and staying there, eyes wide, senses on electrified alert. *That thing that happens to women who were molested as children*, I couldn't stop thinking. *It's happening to me.*

"I cry all the time," I said.

"How much sleep are you getting?"

"One or two hours. Sometimes none."

"Have you gained or lost a significant amount of weight?"

"I've lost ten pounds." The only good thing about this mess was that I was skinny. And—wouldn't you know it?—I was too damn crazy to enjoy it.

Dr. Brill scribbled on the yellow legal pad in her lap. "Any thoughts of hurting yourself?"

I must have mulled this over too long. My silence snapped Dr. Brill out of her trance. She leaned forward in her faux-leather swivel chair, her gawky grasshopper body twitching with sudden urgency. "Do you have a *plan* to hurt yourself?"

If I were capable of planning, I thought, *I wouldn't be here.* "I'm not suicidal," I said.

"Oh," she said, bored again. She was taking my word for it that I wasn't going to kill myself? Who was the crazy person in the room?

"Have you been under any unusual stress?"

"You could say that."

Dr. Brill pushed her glasses up her nose. "Was there an incident that precipitated your insomnia?"

"I had a fight with my father," I said. And then I told her that since that phone call I'd been crying all the time, sleeping almost never, unable to work or drive or eat or cook meals for my kids. I told her that my lover, my best friend, and pretty much every friend and writing student I had was an incest survivor, and that I was pretty sure I was one too. I told her that I felt like I'd fallen through a crack in the earth, and I wasn't sure how or when or if I'd be able to pull myself back up.

Dr. Brill got up, walked to her desk, and pulled a small white pad from a drawer. "I'm giving you a two-month supply of Halcion," she said, handing me a scrip. "But the medication only treats the symptom, not the cause. You really should see a therapist."

I folded the piece of thick white paper into my back pocket. "You're right," I said.

Slightly better living through chemistry: thanks to the Halcion, I was sleeping better, and my insomniac fog had cleared.

But still. I poured my kids' cereal in the morning: *incest breakfast*. Cut their tuna sandwiches into precise halves: *incest lunch*. I walked them to school, and incest chased me home. I worked on my incest pitches and articles, nagged my kids through their homework, *incest*, and their baths—*incest*. If I could have afforded two therapy sessions a day, I would've been wishing for three.

Seemingly undaunted by my previous refusals, Heidi reminded me that co-counseling was free. Beggars couldn't be choosers, and desperate incest survivors couldn't split therapeutic hairs. I signed up for the Re-evaluation Counseling Fundamentals class that promised to transform me into an RC-certified counselor in eight weeks.

The two-hour class met in the living room of a shabby Berkeley clapboard cottage. I hated the whole thing right away. I hated the hideous pillows on the living room floor, and I hated Kathy, the teacher, with her glazed-over face and her threadbare Birkenstocks and her robotically empathic eyes.

I hated the group's bizarre rituals—the therapeutic trifecta that prized shaking, yawning, and sobbing above all else—and its party-line lingo: "present time" and "discharge," *good*; "restimulation" and "distress," *bad*.

I couldn't stand my classmates, either: a motley crew of downwardly mobile eternal hippies in twenty-year-old tie-died T-shirts, they slurped up RC's "liberation theory" like pigs at the trough with a bad case of the munchies.

Most of all, I hated myself.

If I'd had my act together, I wouldn't have had the break-down ("breakthrough," the pathologically positive Kathy called it) that had landed me in this group. If I hadn't had the break-down, I would've spent the past month at my desk instead of in my bed, and I wouldn't have been so broke. If I hadn't been so broke, I would've been able to afford *real* incest therapy. And then there was this. If my father hadn't molested me, I wouldn't have needed incest therapy at all.

But he had. So I did. And so, with only my judgments to shield me from indignities real and imagined, I zipped my opinionated lips and learned the goddamn counseling techniques.

"Emmy and Zach went to Chuck E. Cheese with Grandpa and Granny Gloria," Matthew announced from the backseat.

I was driving the kids home from a weekend at their cousins' house. I'd asked my brother and sister-in-law not to pass infor-mation about me to my father or vice versa, so this was news to me.

"How come we didn't get to go?" Matthew asked.

I hadn't yet said the word "incest" to anyone besides Jane, Heidi, and Dr. Brill. I wasn't about to say it to my kids.

"I'm not sure," I said. Not the truth, exactly, but the smallest lie I could tell.

Did they notice? I wondered. Did my seven- and nine-year-old sons notice that child sexual abuse was in the news as often as it was? I'd never believed in sheltering my kids from what was going on in the world around them, but the TV news lately made even a tell-all mom like me long for parental advisories.

On the NBC Evening News, Tom Brokaw had reported on two Catholic priests, one in Allentown, Pennsylvania, one in Lafayette, Louisiana, both accused of molesting altar boys. The victims' parents were suing the church, claiming that the diocese had known the abuse was going on—for nine years, in one case—

and hadn't done anything to stop it. The guilty priests, the bishop had reportedly said, "will answer to God."

"What's *heinous?*" Matthew asked me.

I told him it was another word for "horrible."

The New York Times
February 29, 1988
"5 Years Changes Much in Child-Molesting Case"

It has been 10 months since the trial began, seven months since the first witness appeared and five years since the child-molesting charges against the McMartin Pre-School hit the courts. And there is no end in sight.

. . . The latest child witness, a slender, 11-year-old boy, took the stand last week . . . mentioning briefly that he once saw Mr. Buckey kill a horse. . . .

The boy, nervous and embarrassed, told of being fondled and forced into oral copulation by Mr. Buckey and said he felt "sick and dirty" when he drew pictures of the incident for his mother.

—AP

Without acknowledging the significance of the date—March 8, International Women's Day—Dan Rather introduced a special report on "incest in the courts" on the CBS Evening News. The story profiled two women who'd filed lawsuits against their childhood molesters.

One woman talked about the lifelong feelings of guilt and humiliation that had provoked her to sue her father. *Guilt and humiliation—check*, I thought. The other woman was shown rehearsing a play she'd written about having been abused by her father and her uncle. Her memories had been repressed until she reached adulthood, and the statute of limitations had run out by the time she decided to sue. The best way to decrease the number of men who molest their children, she said, was to punish the molesters.

In all the years I'd spent being punished by my father, it had never occurred to me that I could punish him. For the first time, I considered suing him for molesting me. I imagined the courtroom scene. My father at the defendant's table next to his lawyer. Me on the witness stand reading from my incest journal. My stomach roiled at the thought.

Am I still protecting him? I asked myself. If I wasn't, wouldn't I have been looking for a way to hurt him as much as he'd hurt me?

The New York Times
March 22, 1988
"Risk of Sex Abuse in Day Care Seen as Lower Than at Home"

A new national study . . . examined substantiated cases of sexual abuse involving 1,639 children at 270 day care facilities across the country.

The researchers estimated that for every 10,000 children enrolled at the centers, 5.5 were sexually abused each year. By contrast they calculated that for every 10,000 preschool children, 8.9 were sexually abused in their homes each year, based on confirmed cases reported to the Government.

People are more likely to report abuse involving those other than their own family members, [Principal Investigator David Finkelhor] added.

—*Warren E. Leary*

In our last co-counseling class, Kathy instructed each of us to choose one of our classmates as our long-term counseling partner. Thank goddess, there was *one* person in the group whom I'd come to like and respect. Catherine and I had so much in common; there couldn't have been a better-matched co-counseling couple than we two.

Catherine and I were both in our late thirties, both moms, both in tumultuous relationships with women. Incredibly, both of us were journalists specializing in sexual abuse. It seemed positively cosmic that while I'd been following the Rand family through treatment at Parents United, Catherine had been in Jordan, Minnesota, interviewing child victims of preschool abuse for a radio series on NPR. We were both eager to feel better, and we were both highly skeptical about the wackiness of RC.

Catherine and I also shared the deepest bond of all. We were both desperate to find proof that our fathers had molested us when we were little girls. With a quick nod exchanged across the room, Catherine and I chose each other.

One night Catherine and I were violating RC's no-socializing clause, hanging out in my kitchen after a session, trading war stories from the trenches of incest journalism. "Doesn't RC seem kind of *cultish* to you?" I asked her.

"I'll say." Catherine laughed mirthlessly. "I can't believe I joined a therapy cult to deal with the fallout from reporting on satanic cults."

She sighed. "When I was working on a feminist film project in L.A. last year," she said, "the crew was kind of cultish, too. They were all incest survivors, and they're the ones who got me thinking I'm one too."

"Sometimes I think that's all life is," Catherine said. "Trading in one belief system, one cult, for the next."

The Washington Post
June 30, 1988
"Law Allowing Children to Testify Behind Screens Is Nullified"

The Supreme Court struck down yesterday an Iowa law permitting children who say they are victims of sexual abuse to testify behind screens.

The court, in a ruling that was written by Justice Antonin Scalia, said use of the screen violated the defendant's Sixth Amendment right to confront witnesses against him.

...As the number of child sex-abuse cases has grown in recent years, states have grappled with how to protect child witnesses without violating the confrontation clause.

—*Ruth Marcus*

My father's sixty-first birthday was July 18. I thought about not calling him and it hurt. I thought about calling him and it hurt.

Was it my fifth birthday or my tenth, the night my dad took me to Mama Leone's, that midtown Manhattan midcentury cavern of kitsch, and told me to order one or two or three of whatever I wanted because "You're the birthday girl"?

Were my mother and my brother at the table when I ordered my favorite Italian dish, spaghetti with clam sauce—red, not white, because my dad and I liked our clam sauce and clam chowder red?

Was it really just my father and me to whom a procession of waiters delivered my birthday surprise, a giant ball of spumoni melting beneath the heat of five—or was it ten—sputtering candles?

My mother and my brother must have been there; my father wouldn't have taken me out for my birthday dinner alone. But all I could remember was my dad, my dad, my dad who loved me so much, who made me feel like a princess, my dad who'd arranged the whole glittering night: the waiters singing "Thank Heaven for Little Girls," everyone in the restaurant craning their necks to smile at me, singing along.

For the first time ever, in 1988 I didn't send him a birthday card.

The Miami Herald
July 22, 1988
"Ex-Educator Faces More Sex Charges"

The state attorney's office filed 16 additional charges against Montessori educator James Herbertson Toward on Thursday in connection with alleged sexual assaults on five former students of his private Stuart school. Seventeen children have been listed in court records as potential victims in the case.

My thirty-seventh birthday was August 21. Despite my failure to acknowledge his, as always, my father sent me a Hallmark card. As always, he signed it "Love, Dad."

Heidi gave me a fitting birthday gift: a copy of a new book everyone was reading, *The Courage to Heal*.

Neve:
I know you have

THE COURAGE

TO HEAL

I love you —
Heidi

The book was amazing, full of personal stories and checklists and great advice. Reading it helped me with my most important project: learning to believe myself.

> Forgetting is one of the most common and effective ways children deal with sexual abuse. The human mind has tremendous powers of repression. Many children are able to forget about the abuse, even as it is happening to them.

> It is natural that you have periodic doubts of your experience. But that's because accepting memories is painful, not because you weren't abused.

> Total obsession with sexual abuse is more likely if you've forgotten your abuse.

> To say, "I was abused," you don't need the kind of recall that would stand up in a court of law.

Everywhere I went I saw those big purple letters on that stark white cover: in all of our therapists' waiting rooms, on friends' coffee tables, on the New Nonfiction shelf at my local bookstore, at the neighborhood public library.

I scoured the book, notepad and yellow Post-its in hand, making a list of symptoms that matched mine, flagging family dynamics and childhood stories that reminded me of my own. I brought it to my next session with Catherine and set it in front of her, dotted with yellow flags: exhibits 1 through infinity in the case against my dad.

"Have you seen this book?" I asked.

"I'm in it," she answered.

She turned to page 88 and read her quote out loud. "It was like there were six-foot-high letters in my living room every day when I woke up: *INCEST!*"

For a couple of years before we'd met, Catherine told me, she'd been in an incest survivor's support group with Laura Davis, the book's coauthor. "I was in that exploring phase," Catherine said. "I had memories I was trying to work through. It was agonizing work, and I wasn't sure I was right."

When Laura asked to interview her for the book, Catherine had spent several sleepless nights worrying that her father would come after her and kill her if she agreed. Finally she'd decided to be interviewed, and to use her real name. "I hoped my agony might do someone else some good," she told me.

We set the timer to start our session. Catherine asked to go first.

"I'm five years old," she said, facing me on my couch, her eyes burning, her hands trembling in mine. "A man gets into bed with me. He puts something inside me. It hurts."

"It hurts," I repeated, giving her the mirroring she needed.

"My father hurt me," she sobbed.

"Yes," I said, validating her feelings. "He did."

When it was my turn, I read her the list I'd been keeping.

WHAT MAKES ME THINK I WAS MOLESTED

1. Croup - age 18 months - holding my breath til I turned blue; deciding whether to live or die

2. Nosebleeds - ages 4 on? - waking up in the night with blood everywhere

3. Constant nightmares and insomnia - always. The dream: a monster is in my bedroom, I run for the door, my feet are stuck to the floor, a scream is stuck in my throat...

23. He married a woman my age.

24. He had a terrible sexual relationship with and hated my mother.

25. The dreams

"My father hurt me," I sobbed.

"Yes," Catherine said, mirroring me, validating my feelings. "He did."

Journal entry, August 30, 1988

I want to try to honor my feelings of sadness because I know
they're about INCEST. As Catherine's quote in the incest book
says—it's like that word is written in 6-foot letters in the living
room every day.

Jane added Rosen bodywork to her therapy schedule. She was
seeing her individual therapist on Mondays, our couple's counselor with me on Tuesdays, and her Rosen bodyworker on
Thursdays.

I'd asked Jane whether it was worth the two hundred bucks
a week. She'd answered categorically. She couldn't function
without therapy, she said, so how would she earn a living if she
stopped? "I can barely function even *with* it," she'd said.

I didn't dare say so, but all that therapy didn't seem to be
helping. Jane was more fearful, more easily "triggered" than
ever. Everything "brought up her memories" of being molested:
a tiny earthquake, a fender-bender, Matthew and Charlie growing taller.

But who was I to talk? My co-counseling didn't seem to be
helping much, either. I'd heard the "healing crisis" theory of
incest recovery: that feeling worse was a necessary step toward
feeling better. But I couldn't stand the way I felt. If I was going
to be a decent mother to my children, a decent lover to Jane, a
decent journalist, a decent human being, professional therapy
wasn't an option anymore. It was a necessity.

I called a couple of incest therapists I'd interviewed, and
asked for a referral. Both recommended Ruth, whose office was
a short bike ride from my house.

And in a house: a homey Berkeley brown shingle cottage, its
waiting room well stocked with the requisite *The New Yorkers*,
served with a twist of *The Atlantic*.

I liked Ruth as soon as I saw her—her graying hair; flowing,
stylish clothes; warm, intelligent blue eyes. As she showed me

into her office I saw that it was decorated in my favorite color combination, dusty pink and grey. An R. C. Gorman print hung on the wall, the same print that hung on mine.

Liking Ruth, feeling comfortable with her, made me want to flee. "My father molested me when I was little," I said, scrutinizing her face. Was that a flicker of doubt in her eyes?

"I'm sorry that happened to you," Ruth said—sincerely or doubtfully, I couldn't tell.

I pulled out my journal and presented the evidence: my list of symptoms, my memories, my dreams. "I couldn't have had this many dreams about something that didn't happen," I said.

Ruth said nothing.

"Could I have?" I asked.

"What matters is what *you* think," Ruth said, and then she sat there just looking at me.

I sat there looking back at her, remembering the other recurring dreams of my life. Flying (embarrassingly trite). My teeth falling out (textbook insecurity). Being chased by the police because I've murdered my mother (paging Doctor Freud).

I didn't like the way it made me feel, realizing that I'd had symbolic, fictitious dreams before. But just because I'd never sprouted wings, lost all my teeth, or killed my mother didn't mean my incest dreams weren't true.

I'd spent years kicking my way up from the dark depths of doubt. I didn't want to sink back into that muck.

"I *know* my father molested me," I said.

"You sound quite sure of that," Ruth said.

I felt a rush of anger. For this cheap therapy trick I was paying eighty bucks? Catherine mirrored me for free.

"I *am* sure of that," I said. But I felt like a rebellious teenager saying it. The words tasted tinny in my mouth. "Pretty sure," I added.

Suddenly I was furious. Which only proved my point. *The Courage to Heal* called anger "the backbone of healing."

If I wasn't an incest survivor, I couldn't have turned so angry this fast. Could I?

I decided to look for another therapist.

"So," Ruth said, "are you here to work on your feelings about being molested by your father?"

"Of course." *I'm an incest survivor. What else would I want to work on?*

"Would you like to tell me about it?"

"About what?"

Ruth regarded me steadily. "About being molested by your father."

"Are you one of those therapists who doesn't believe in recovered memory?" I blurted.

"I'm one of those therapists," she said, "who believes in my clients."

We sat in silence for a long moment. "I don't exactly remember being molested," I admitted. "But that doesn't mean it didn't happen."

"That's true," Ruth said. And waited.

"I want to be sure," I said.

Ruth nodded, her eyes still locked on mine. "Barring a confession from your father," she said, "all you'll ever be sure of is your own truth. But learning to believe yourself might help you more than any answer could."

Don't treat me like an idiot, I thought. "I'm a journalist," I said, drawing myself upright in my pink velvet chair. "I need answers. And I know how to get them."

"This isn't your job we're talking about, Meredith. It's your life," Ruth said. "Can you stand to hang out with not knowing while we explore the issues that got you to this place?"

"I'm *tired* of exploring." My anger evaporated. I started to cry. "It's been *years.* I want to feel better *now.*"

Ruth handed me a box of Kleenex. The new, pretty "decorator" box, not the institutional, boring kind. "Does it help at all to know that I'll accompany you on this journey," she said softly, "no matter how many twists and turns it takes?"

"You talk like a poet," I said.

"I am a poet."

Who isn't a poet? I thought, instantly angry again.

"A published poet," Ruth added, as if she'd read my mind.

A therapist who's a published poet? That's something you don't run across every day. Maybe she and I make a better match than I thought.

When my fifty minutes were up, I made an appointment to see Ruth again the following week. But just to be sure I had something to show for my eighty dollars, I grabbed a handful of Kleenex on my way out the door.

seven

Did He or Didn't He?

An essential part of healing from child sexual
abuse is telling the truth about your life. . . . You
may find that some relationships cannot stand this
challenge and you will grieve for them, along with
your other losses.

—*Ellen Bass and Laura Davis*,
The Courage to Heal, 1988

Jane was at therapy; Matthew and Charlie and I were at the
kitchen table eating dinner. "Emmy and Zach went to a Giants
game with Grandpa and Granny Gloria," Matthew said. "How
come we didn't get to go?"

Charlie chewed a Tater Tot, his lips outlined in ketchup.
"We never see Grandpa and Granny Gloria anymore," he
commented.

I wasn't ready to tell my kids the whole truth, but I didn't
want to lie to them, either.

"I had a fight with Grandpa a few months ago," I said. "That's
why we don't see him anymore."

I hated my half-assed answer: a little bit of truth, a whole lot
of lie. "*We* didn't," Charlie said.

"You didn't what?" I asked.

"We didn't have a fight with Grandpa. Just because *you* don't
feel like seeing him, why can't we?"

"Dad could take us," Matthew added.

What am I teaching my kids about family? I saw myself twenty years from now, distraught because one of my sons was mad at me and wouldn't let me see his kids.

What were my options? Tell more half-truths, tell more lies? Or do what I'd taught my children to do, no matter what?

I shepherded them to the living room couch, still rumpled from that afternoon's tearful session with Catherine. I sat between them, one arm around each boy's shoulders.

"Grandpa Stan hurt me when I was little," I said. "I don't want that to happen to you."

"He spanked you?" Charlie asked.

"That's part of it, yes," I said.

"You slapped me in the face," Charlie said. "In the car. On the way to San Jose. Remember?"

"Yes, honey, I do remember," I said, resisting the urge to do what co-counseling had taught me never to do: try to argue anyone, especially my nine-year-old son, out of his truth. "I'm so sorry I did that, Charlie. I lost my temper. That was wrong."

"But *I* still have to talk to *you*," Charlie said.

The truth, the whole truth, and nothing but the truth? "Grandpa hurt me in other ways, too," I said. "I don't want you guys to see him because I want to keep you safe."

The boys pondered this. I could feel their minds straining to embrace what I'd said.

"What about Emmy and Zach?" Matthew said. "They see Grandpa and Granny all the time. How come Doug and Susie aren't keeping *them* safe?"

I swallowed hard. "Parents don't always agree about what's best for their kids."

I pulled the boys closer. At nine and ten, they were still cuddly, but not tonight. Their bodies stiffened against my touch.

Who's the monster, I thought.

Sitting on Ruth's pink velvet couch, I opened my copy of *The Courage to Heal*, flipped to the page I'd marked with a Post-it, and read a passage to Ruth. "It was only when Emily broke off all communication with her family and established a consistent relationship with a skilled therapist who believed her that she stopped doubting herself and got on with her recovery."

"What is it you want me to understand?" Ruth asked.

"I broke off communication with my father. I established a consistent relationship with a skilled therapist," I said. "So why can't I stop doubting myself and get on with my recovery already?"

Ruth waited, smiling at me, as if she were absolutely confident that we were going to solve this mystery, that I *would* get on with my recovery somehow. But why wouldn't she just tell me whether my father had molested me or not?

"I'm sorry I can't give you the answer you're looking for." Ruth leaned forward in her chair. "But I'm not holding out on you, Meredith. I honestly don't know what's true for you."

"If you don't, who does?" I said.

Ruth's blue eyes softened. Before she could give me her usual annoying answer, I said, "Don't answer that."

Jane and I waited in a long line to see *The Good Mother*, the film based on the Sue Miller novel we'd devoured when it came out in 1986.

Diane Keaton played Anna, a young mother in the throes of sexual awakening. Liam Neeson played Leo, her freethinking man. When Anna's three-year-old daughter asked to touch Leo's penis in the shower, he let her. Anna's ex-husband charged Anna with being an unfit mother, sued for full custody, and won.

"That's what a woman always gets for having great sex," I commented as we were driving home. "Punished."

"You think what the mother did was *okay*?" Jane said.

"She didn't do anything wrong. Neither did her boyfriend. The ex-husband and the judge were prudes."

"The boyfriend sexually abused the little girl," Jane argued. "The mother didn't protect her. The judge was right to take her daughter away."

And then we were off and running. Same as always, what we were really fighting about was which of us was more victimized as a child and therefore had the greater need to be taken care of, heard and empowered and believed.

It was Jane. Always Jane. Because despite the fact that my father had molested me, I was so much less damaged than Jane, who'd started recovering memories of being abused not only by her brother and her father but also by a satanic cult.

And so when I hurled the accusation at Jane that she'd hurled so often and so effectively at me—"How can you treat me this way, *when you know what I'm going through?*"—I knew it wouldn't get me what I wanted. It was never going to be my turn. Jane would always be the more wounded one.

The New York Times
October 13, 1988
"Judge in Case of Child Abuse Dismisses Some of Charges"

The judge in the long trial of two people accused of sexually abusing children at the McMartin Pre-School dismissed more than a quarter of the charges today because three child witnesses refused to testify for the prosecution. . . . The trial, before Judge William Pounders, has already lasted 15 months.

—*Reuters*

Their homework done, Matthew and Charlie had earned an hour of pre-bedtime TV. Channel-surfing, we happened on a two-hour Geraldo Rivera special: *Devil Worship: Exploring Satan's Underground*.

"What's Satan?" Charlie asked.

"It's another word for the devil," Matthew said.

"The very young and impressionable should definitely not be watching this program tonight," Rivera declared. "This is not a Halloween fable."

Hearing this, Matthew and Charlie assumed the we're-so-watching-this position. I commandeered the remote and changed the channel.

"Mo-o-om," they wailed.

"That show's for grown-ups," I said.

"But it's *educational*," Matthew said, giving it the old grade-school try.

"Some things," I said, "you don't need to be educated about."

I hope.

The Miami Herald
December 29, 1988
"Child's Parents Sue in Sex-Abuse Case"

Stuart—Parents of another child who allegedly was subjected to sexual abuse at the old Glendale Montessori School have filed a civil suit in Martin County Circuit Court. James Toward, 57, former director of the school, and Brenda Williams, 29, his secretary, face multiple criminal charges of sexual battery, kidnapping and lewd and lascivious assault on at least 12 young students.

I couldn't keep it to myself anymore. It was time to tell my family the truth.

I'd wanted to be absolutely certain before I made my accusation public. But, as Ruth kept reminding me, there was no guarantee that day would ever come. Besides, as *The Courage to Heal* said, I needed all the support and validation I could get.

I asked my brother to meet me for dinner at a dive seafood joint in a dive town halfway between his house and mine. I didn't want to have that conversation in a restaurant we'd ever want to visit again.

Crumbling crackers into lumpy white chowder, more cornstarch than clams, we sat facing each other across a greasy Formica table beneath a mural of cavorting whales and porpoises. "What's the difference between a dolphin and a porpoise?" I mused, stalling.

"What I want to know is, what's the *porpoise* of this meeting?" I heard my father in my brother's dumb pun. I felt a pang of missing my father, and a memory surfaced: my father standing on the edge of a motel pool, yelling "Jump! Jump!" at three-year-old me, his way of teaching me to swim.

I jumped. "I'm pretty sure Dad molested me," I said.

My brother's spoon clattered onto the table. "*What?*"

I pulled out my list, "What Makes Me Think I Was Molested," and read it to my brother. I watched him wrestling with what I was saying. In thirty-two years of being his big sister, I'd never seen him look so miserable.

"I've read your articles," he said finally. "I know this kind of thing happens all the time. I just never thought—"

"I know," I said. "Me neither."

"So why—?"

"It took me a long time and a lot of therapy to put the clues together," I said. "But there's no other way it all makes sense."

"I know Jane was . . . ," he couldn't quite say the word. "And Heidi. Are you sure you're not just . . ."

"You think I'm being *peer-pressured* into accusing Dad of molesting me?"

"I'm just asking. Doesn't that seem weird to you? Your girl-friend. Your best friend. Now you."

Tears sprang to my eyes. I couldn't handle this without Doug. "It's shocking to me, too," I said. "But I really need you to believe me."

"I do," my brother said. "I do believe you."

My sister-in-law called me at seven the next morning. "I'm so sorry, Mer," she said. "Is there anything I can do?"

I felt drenched in relief. All those horror stories in *The Courage to Heal*, all those incest survivors being disbelieved by their families: that wasn't happening to me. "Thank you so much for asking," I said. "I'll let you know if I think of anything."

Susie hesitated. "I'm sorry, but I need to ask you something."

She doesn't really believe me, I thought, bracing myself.

"Doug and I were talking," she went on. "Do you think it's safe to leave Emmy and Zach alone with your dad?"

I saw beaming Emmy and innocent Zach with my boys in my father's apartment: laughing at my dad's bad jokes, eating the best potstickers in town, drinking forbidden cans of Pepsi, watching horse races on my father's big, fancy TV.

I'm ruining my family, I thought. *And I'm not even sure why.*

Believe yourself, I heard my lover and my best friend and my therapists saying. *If you think you were abused and your life shows the symptoms, then you were.*

"No," I told my sister-in-law. "I wouldn't leave your kids with him if I were you."

A week later I came home to a message from my father on my answering machine. "Emmy's telling some crazy story about me hurting you, Meredith. What the hell is this about?"

My hand shook as I pressed Erase. *He can't punish me anymore*, I told myself. But fear—*or was it remorse?*—pounded through me.

Journal entry, December 12, 1988

My dream:

I'm counseling Catherine and she's berating herself because she slept with someone besides her girlfriend once.

She's saying how she's just as bad as her father—who molested her—because she did this awful thing, she lied to her girlfriend. I'm pleading with her to see the difference between what he did and what she did . . . and I get a visual image of a father standing next to an infant's crib, looking down at a baby, thinking how he could make it okay that he was about to put his finger inside her.

Ten years ago, shortly after Emmy's birth, my mother had moved to an apartment a mile from my house. It was a place I seldom went.

Since she'd arrived in Berkeley, my mother had become a professor of international law and a well-known human rights activist. But as much as I appreciated her progressive politics, as much as I admired her unflagging energy and her intellectual curiosity, our relationship remained as tortured as it had always been.

Now, finally, I understood why. Anticipating a conversation about the past had brought my oldest hopes to the surface. Once we talked about what had really come between us, I fantasized, my mother would love me the way I'd always wanted her to, I'd love my mother the way I'd always wished I had. How *could* we have been close? Incest had turned me into her sexual competitor. Maybe now we could finally unsnarl our mother-daughter knot.

I made a date to see her. I brought Jane along. My mother hugged me, stiffly as always, and then she hugged Jane the same way. We sat at her round dining room table, perched on the edges of our chairs. Jane nodded at me, her eyes radiating love.

"I need to tell you something," I said. "Something no mother wants to hear." I had a sudden vision of myself and Jane as soldiers in a vast incest survivors' army. I saw dozens, hundreds, thousands of other women behind me, saying these same words to their mothers with the same grief in their hearts and the same fire in their guts.

My mother paled. I knew what she was thinking. Since her diagnosis with breast cancer in 1977, she'd told me often how worried she was that cancer would be her legacy to me.

"I think Dad molested me," I said. "I mean, I'm pretty sure he did."

My mother's mouth dropped open. Her lips moved, but no sound emerged.

I jumped out of my chair and stood behind her, wrapped my arms around her chest. She reached up to me, leaned back into me, grabbed my hands where they crossed her heart.

Finally. My mother's cheek was so soft against mine. This was what I'd ached for as long as I'd been alive. *If all this pain brings my mother and me together, at least one good thing will have come out of it.*

"When you were two years old," my mother said shakily, "he told me you looked too sexy in your bathing suit. He was so angry. His reaction sickened me. I didn't know why."

Oh, my God, I thought. *It's true. I really am an incest survivor.*

"I didn't know why," my mother said again. She reached around and pulled me into her lap, the place I'd always yearned to be. "How could I have let this happen to my baby?" she wept.

"It wasn't your fault, Mom," I said, bursting with love for my mother. *Finally. Finally.* "You didn't know."

My mother and I sobbed in each other's arms. *I've wanted this forever. And now here it is. Here it is.*

"I love you, Mom," I said. Suddenly her body arched against mine, ejecting me from her lap.

"What you're saying is impossible," my mother said. "Your father couldn't have done that to you. He didn't even like sex with *me*."

I shot Jane a desperate look. *Don't panic*, Jane's blue eyes told me. *She's just heard the worst news a mother can hear. She'll come around.*

I leaned in close to my mother. "It happens all the time, Mom," I said, in my calmest co-counseling voice. "A lot of men who like sex with little girls don't like sex with their wives."

"I always hated the way you and your father ganged up on me," she said.

"Of course you did," I said.

My mirroring wasn't working on my mother. She glared at me. "How can you do this?" she said. "How can you tell such a hideous lie?"

I burst into tears. So much for detachment.

Jane got up and stood behind me, rested her hands on my shoulders. "She's not lying," she told my mother. "I know this is hard for you. But she's your daughter. Please remember—it's hard for her, too."

"I just can't believe it." My mother started crying again, not looking at Jane, not looking at me.

A moment ago my mother and I had been one. Now I was behind a one-way mirror watching my mother. I could see and hear her, but she couldn't see or hear me.

"I can't believe it," she said again, her head in her hands.

"All you can know is your truth," I heard Ruth saying. But what I was saying didn't feel like truth. It felt like a cancer. *I* felt like a cancer, poisoning everyone I loved. I'd made my lifelong recurrent nightmare—*I'm running from the police; they're chasing me because I killed my mother*—come true.

I take it back, I wanted to say. *I was wrong.*

Was I? Or did I want to take my accusation back because telling the truth was causing more harm than being molested ever had?

I leaned over and put my arms around my mother. She sat upright, pushing me away.

"We're going now," I said. Jane gathered up our jackets, put her arm around me, led me to the front door. When we got there I turned around, still hoping. But my mother's back was to me. Her shoulders were shaking. I wanted to run to her, comfort her, tell her I'd made it all up. And I wanted her to run to me, comfort me, tell me how sorry she was.

"I'll call you tomorrow, Mom," I said, feeling like a victim, feeling like a perpetrator. I was driving this train, and I was tied up on the tracks in front of it. I couldn't stop it now.

My mother called me first thing the next morning.

"I'm glad you told me about your . . . feelings," she said in measured, distant tones. "And I'm really sorry you've been in such pain."

She believes me. Again that strange mix: horror, relief.

"But now that you've gotten this off your chest," she continued, "can't we just move on? Put the past behind us?"

"I *want* to put the past behind me," I said. "But I need to understand it first."

"While you're trying to understand your past," my mother said, "innocent people are getting hurt."

"Innocent people?"

"Your father had his failings. But there's no way he could have done something like that to you." She paused. When she spoke again, her voice was hoarse, her words deliberate. "He loved you more than anyone else in the world."

That's what's wrong between my mother and me. She's been jealous of me since the day I was born.

But why?

Because her husband was having sex with me? Or because he loved me more than he loved her?

She's my mother, and she's in pain, and it's my fault.

"I'm sorry this is so hard on you," I said.

"This isn't about how I feel," my mother interrupted me. "This is about the truth."

She was right. But whose?

"The truth is," I said, "a lot of fathers love the daughters they molest."

"Not yours," my mother said.

Who could know my father, and my childhood, better than my own mother?

I could. I do. My mother has never really known me or my father. That's the cause of this whole catastrophe.

"I've got to get the kids up," I said. "They're going to be late for school."

"I hope you'll think about what I'm telling you," my mother said.

"Believe me, Mom," I said, "I will."

The Gainesville Sun
December 29, 1988
"Children Change Stories in Montessori Abuse Case"

The attorney for a former Montessori school owner accused of sexually abusing students says five of the six alleged victims have changed their stories or admitted inventing the allegations.

James Toward, 58, and his former office manager, Brenda Williams, 29, were arrested in March on charges they kidnapped and sexually abused a 4-year-old boy at the Glendale Montessori School. They are being held without bail in the Martin County Jail. . . .

"None of them are saying anything even close to what was in the initial reports," Toward's attorney . . . said. "In some cases, they've admitted making up the entire story."

Journal entry, March 14, 1989

My dream:

Mom is crying. I know it's because Dad hurt her, sexually. I start yelling at Dad, "What are you doing to her? Are you doing it to <u>her</u>, now, too?" He's <u>furious</u>.

I'm thinking, "Now my brother & sister-in-law will see it's all true, everything I've been telling them."

I start yelling at Dad, "You son of a bitch." I'm pounding on his chest with my fists.

"Hello, Meredith," my father's wife said. My hand tightened on the phone.

"I need to talk to you," she said. "Can we meet for lunch?"

"Of course," I said. *It's the least I can do,* I thought.

As soon as we were seated, Gloria began to cry. "If your father really molested you," she said through her tears, "I have to divorce him. I can't live with a pedophile."

The enormity of what I'd done—what I was still doing—hit me in a way it hadn't before. Was I really willing to destroy the happiest of my father's three marriages, to take the weeping woman in front of me prisoner in a war in which she'd played no part?

In that moment I made a choice: to overrule my doubts, to claim a certainty I didn't quite own. *If his wife thinks it's possible,* I told myself, *it must be true.* "I can't tell you what to do about your marriage," I said. "All I can tell you is what I believe."

"And you believe your father sexually abused you," Gloria said.

"Yes," I meant to say. "No," I heard myself saying. "I *suspect* that he molested me."

Gloria stared at me, confused. Streaks of mascara striped her cheeks. "What are you saying, Meredith? Should I leave him or not?"

If his wife thinks it's possible, it must be true.

"I can't answer that," I said.

We sat in silence. "I'm sorry," I said, feeling like the world's worst human being. Or would that be my father, the child molester?

Gloria stared at me for a long moment. Then, still crying, she got up and left.

I drove back across San Francisco Bay, back to Planet Incest, where the question was always incest and the answer was always incest and the explanation for everything was always incest, and no one ever asked, "Are you sure?"

The Miami Herald
March 31, 1989
"Firm: Insurance Won't Cover Abuse"

A former Montessori schoolteacher's insurance company doesn't want to pay damages to parents of children the man allegedly molested. The United States Fidelity and Guaranty Co., which insured James Toward, his wife, Rosario, and their Glendale Montessori School, filed suit in U.S. District Court in Fort Lauderdale on Thursday asking that the company be relieved from paying any money that might be awarded to parents who are suing Toward.

The 7.1 Loma Prieta earthquake of 1989 shook Jane and me emotionally as well as seismically. "If not now, when?" was the answer to every question. After six years of living apart, we bought a house big enough for Jane to have her own little world in the attic, the kids to have their own rooms, and a sun-drenched office for me.

On the day Jane and I made an offer on that house, my father left a message on my answering machine. How could he have known? How did he always know?

"Hello, Meredith," he said in his I'm-in-charge-here, don't-even-think-about-disobeying-me voice. "I'm wondering if you're ready to resume our relationship."

I didn't call him back, of course. But shutting my father out of my life didn't shut him out of my head. For once, Ruth had a practical suggestion. "Have you thought of writing him a letter?" she asked.

I was stunned by this travesty. "The last thing I want is to be in touch with him," I said.

"I'm talking about being in touch with yourself," Ruth said. "I didn't say you had to send it."

Journal entry, May 31, 1989

Dad,

Here is why I don't want to see you. Because when I start to write this I feel fear clutching at my stomach and sexual feeling clutching at my genitals.

I don't want to see you because I've spent the time since I haven't seen or spoken to you working on incest. Incest between you and me. Perpetrated by you.

The hard reality, Dad, is that you hurt me in ways I might spend the rest of my life uncovering and recovering from. And that is the core of the pain that is in me from you. You have never accepted the role of father (you) to child (me). . . .

I was okay until I wouldn't be your mirror, wasn't I? When I would play baseball with you and "inherit" your writing skill and eat hamburgers for breakfast with you and keep secrets from my mother with you.

And what else did you need me for? And what else did you use me for?

I don't want to see you because I'm afraid I'm not strong enough to defend my truth in the face of yours.

So this is not a question but a firm statement: I want you to stay away from me—physically and psychically—and stay away from my children, until such time that you are ready to be a father to me, or never, whichever comes first.

Your daughter,
Meredith

I didn't send the letter.

The Miami Herald
June 15, 1989
"Ex-Owner of School Guilty of Sex Abuse"

Former Glendale Montessori School owner James Toward cut short his scheduled trial Wednesday on charges that he sexually abused children in his care by pleading guilty to reduced counts in an agreement with prosecutors.

While remaining calm through the proceedings and continuing to maintain his innocence, Toward, 58, immediately was sentenced to 27 years in prison and 10 years probation.

eight

In Therapy We Trust

"You can't imagine how many calls I get from people with the same story," the therapist told us on the phone during the summer of 1991.

"Well, then, please have them contact us," we replied. And you did.

It is our numbers that will let the world know how widespread this nonsense has become. This nonsense has devastated us: lawsuits, deaths, divorces, broken families, heartbreak.
—FMS Foundation Newsletter, *Vol. 1, No. 1,*
March 15, 1992

The longest, most expensive trial in American history, the trial that had engendered so many others, had come to an end. But the questions that had sparked it remained unanswered.

People Magazine
February 5, 1990
"The McMartin Nightmare: California's Notorious Sexual Abuse Trial Ends in Acquittal, Leaving a Legacy of Anger and Anguish"

On Jan. 18, after nine weeks of deliberation, an exhausted and emotionally drained Los Angeles Superior Court jury acquitted the

Buckeys on 52 counts—and found itself deadlocked on 13 others.
But that acquittal came late indeed for the defendants, whose lives
lay in tatters.

...Even more wrenching was the stunned disbelief of the children
who claimed—and were surely convinced—that they had been
molested. Many of these boys and girls had spent more than half their
lives in a nightmarish legal battle that ended, for them, in despair.
"There was a little scream of terror in the room when the verdicts
were read," said Kyle Daniels, 14, one of nine children who testified
at the trial.

"...I'm angry they let those guys off and angry at the Buckeys
for what they did," [said K. C. Wachs, 11, who told Manhattan
Beach police in 1983 that she had been forced to perform sex acts
by the Buckeys]. "They are perverts and now they're back on the
street."

—Susan Schindehette

Two years after I'd stopped speaking to my father, my kids
and I were at my brother's house, and I walked by Emmy's
room and overheard a conversation between her and my
older son.

Emmy was seven months old when I gave birth to Matthew,
and she'd spent several of my thirty-six hours of labor crawling
around on my bucking belly. She'd been Matthew's first and
favorite playmate; the two of them had been like siblings since.
At eleven years old, little between them went unsaid.

"Where'd you get the camera?" I heard Matthew say.

After a long, uncharacteristic silence, Matthew said, "Oh.
Did Granny and Grandpa buy it for you?"

"Uh-huh," Emmy said, and I heard it all in their voices: his
envy and longing. Her sorrow and survivor's guilt.

My kids were eleven and ten years old. Too old to be molested
by my father and not tell me about it. On the drive home that

night, I told Matthew and Charlie that I wasn't ready to spend time with my father, but that if they wanted to see him and Granny Gloria, I'd make it happen.

"Will it hurt your feelings if we say yes?" Charlie asked.

My chest ached. "Honey," I said, "I didn't keep you from seeing your grandfather because of *my* feelings. I did it because I didn't want him to hurt *you*."

"How come you don't think he'll hurt us anymore?" Matthew asked.

I tried to imagine my father—my nervous, hilarious, narcissistic father—molesting my children. The notion was inconceivable. So how could I believe that he'd done that to me?

Not for the first time, I yearned to take it all back, to tell my kids and my father and the rest of my family that I was sorry, that I'd made a terrible mistake.

"You're older now," I said. "If I thought he would hurt you, I wouldn't let you go."

"I want to see them," Matthew said. His eagerness wrenched me.

"Me too," Charlie added quickly, with that second-child anxiety of his that always reminded me of my dad, also a younger brother.

I asked my ex-husband if he'd take the boys to see my father. The two of them had never gotten along, of course; my father had treated Robert the way he'd treated every other man in my life.

"I know he's the only grandfather they've got," Robert said. "But if he's a child molester, I don't want the kids to have anything to do with him. And I don't want anything to do with him myself."

"They really want to see him," I said, trying not to sound as defensive as I felt. "And if you stay with them the whole time..."

"I'll think about it," Robert said.

A week later, he and his girlfriend invited my father and Gloria over for dinner. A few weeks after that, Robert drove

Matthew and Charlie to Chinatown to meet my father, and they all went out for dim sum.

Both times when the kids got home, I asked if they'd had a good time. Both times they were uncharacteristically taciturn. Both times panic rose up in me, the taste of gunmetal in my mouth. Were my kids keeping secrets to protect my father? Burying memories that would come back to haunt them decades from now?

Soon enough, my father's short attention span kicked in and the question became moot. My father stopped calling Robert to talk to Matthew and Charlie, and Matthew and Charlie stopped asking Robert to take the kids to see my dad.

Who'd lost interest in whom? The end of the short-lived grandfather-grandson reunion seemed mutual to me. Maybe my kids were too old to bond with a grandfather they'd never really known. Maybe my dad was too self-absorbed to maintain interest in a couple of preadolescents, spawn of his raging daughter to boot. After all, if my father had ever been able to put his kids' needs ahead of his own gratification, he wouldn't have lost contact with his grandsons, or his daughter, in the first place.

In May my father sent Charlie a birthday check for $75, folded neatly inside a Hallmark card signed "Love, Grandpa and Granny Gloria." In December he sent Matthew a similar card, with a check for the same amount, signed the same way.

By 1990 I'd been following the instructions in *The Courage to Heal* for two years, with negligible results. I decided to try a different way to heal.

When Catherine moved to D.C., I put incest into a box and locked it and threw away the key. I stopped writing incest articles and reading incest books and writing in my incest journal and hanging out with incest survivors exclusively. I quit therapy cold turkey, got a regular job at a local firm, writing fundraising letters for nonprofits. I started doing regular things with regular people:

shopping with old and new friends, cheerful friends; going out for drinks after work and to movies that made me laugh instead of cry. I sang along to Michael Jackson instead of the achy, angry wimmin's music of Ferron and Holly Near.

It worked—for me. No more incest dreams, no more sleepless nights, no more crippling depression—for me. There was just one thing about Planet Incest that I couldn't avoid: my lover was still living there. As my nightmares and memories receded, Jane's were becoming more graphic and disturbing. She upped her appointments with her incest therapist to two, three, sometimes four sessions a week.

From this new distance I felt sorry for Jane, not deliciously one with her the way I used to feel. I felt sorry for myself, too. I found myself envying my coworkers' ordinary marriages, their predictable routines and mundane miseries. I'd hoped that living with Jane would make our relationship less tumultuous, more domesticated, but it hadn't. I'd hoped that taking a break from my own incest work would make me more patient with Jane's, but it hadn't. I'd hoped that my determination to live a lighter life would be contagious, but so far, it hadn't been.

Truth be told, I wished Jane would get over it already. But that wasn't something I could say. So I went on being her hero, or trying to be. And she went on remembering.

Shaking in my arms, Jane remembered being raped before she was five years old. She remembered men and women standing around a campfire in a forest, chanting in a strange language, wearing dark robes. She remembered them digging a deep hole. They might have killed a baby, she told me in a child's tremulous voice, and buried it in the hole.

Jane signed up for a karate class, the better to protect herself. The class met three nights a week.

On one of those nights, when the kids were in their rooms pretending to do their homework, I watched an episode of the Geraldo Rivera show called *Investigating Multiple Personalities:*

Did the Devil Make Them Do It? Geraldo introduced his first guest, Kathleen, who claimed to have eight hundred personalities. Next to Kathleen was Kayla, also known as Ellie.

"How are you?" Geraldo asked Kayla/Ellie.

"I'm six now," she replied.

Geraldo looked into the camera, his moustache quivering with outrage. "There are more than twelve hundred guests on my panel today," he said, "all embodied in these three women . . . women with terrifying tales of Multiple Personality Disorder, of human sacrifices and of other unspeakable acts. These ladies say the devil made them this way."

The devil, Geraldo explained, was incest and satanic cult abuse: the same devil that was making me wonder if I needed a couple's counselor or an exorcist. The same devil that was tearing Jane and me apart.

Suddenly there were dozens of preschool satanic ritual abuse cases in American courts, and thousands (or tens of thousands, or hundreds of thousands) of adult daughters claiming to have recovered memories of their fathers' sexual abuse.

There also was a confusing counterforce growing. The people in it were waging war against the memories and the therapists of daughters like me—and the doubts they were expressing weren't so different from my own.

The backlash was being led by an organization of two hundred parents whose name alone made me shiver: the False Memory Syndrome Foundation (FMSF). Its leaders were math professor Peter Freyd and education instructor Pamela Freyd. The couple had formed the group after their thirty-something daughter, Jennifer, remembered in therapy that her father had sexually abused her.

The senior Freyds had denied her accusation in the most public, hostile—*or desperate, heartbroken*—way.

The pendulum's swing had slowed. It seemed to be settling near center.

FMS Foundation Newsletter
March 15, 1992
Vol. I, No. I

Has your grown child falsely accused you as a consequence of repressed "memories"? You are not alone. Please help us document the scope of this problem. Contact: 1-800-568-8882.

Request from a Family
Are you or have you been involved in a lawsuit brought on the basis of recovery of repressed "memories"? We are being sued by our daughter, and we would like to network with others in the same or similar situations.
. . . FMS will not release names or material of members. . . . If you wish to reply to this family, please write to FMS.

Maybe it was the power of the FMSF, many of whose members were pillar-of-their-community types, and whose scientific and professional advisory board included high-visibility experts like memory expert Elizabeth Loftus, Freud critic Frederick Crews, and Johns Hopkins psychiatrist Paul McHugh.

Maybe the country was going through another one of its periodic reversals about the existence of child sexual abuse.

Or maybe the outlandishness of some of the charges in some of the abuse cases had sparked the same skepticism that had begun to plague me. Whatever the reason, suddenly the same newspapers and TV shows and bookstores whose pages and airwaves and shelves had been brimming with preschool abuse and incest stories were jumping on the false memory syndrome bandwagon. It wasn't even an actual syndrome, FMSF's critics argued; it was just a phrase that the FMSF had made up.

Soon after the FMSF published its first newsletter, *60 Minutes* aired an exposé of the charges against a Washington couple, Bill and Kathy Swan, who'd been imprisoned since a worker at their daughter's child-care center accused them of molesting their own three-year-old daughter. "It was not until after the Swans were convicted," host Morley Safer said, "that details about [their accuser] began to emerge. She has a history of making bizarre allegations. She told freelance reporter Dean Huber she'd made at least twenty earlier accusations of child abuse. She said she'd been a drug addict, an alcoholic, and that she'd been abused since the age of five by hundreds of men."

The show sent a clear message that the Swans were innocent and should be released. But given the past—the country's, mine—I found that message hard to swallow whole.

The New York Times
January 3, 1993
"Beware the Incest-Survivor Machine

To want to throw a small wrench into the abuse-survivor machine is like opposing censorship of pornography: nowadays, you feel you have to apologize for any support you might be providing to molesters, rapists, pedophiles and other misogynists. This . . . results from the terrible polarization that has emerged on the subject of the sexual abuse of children.

One side, primarily committed to protecting children, emphasizes the appalling prevalence of the abuse of children and the tendency of adults, in every generation, to deny or diminish the reality of this abuse. The other side, primarily committed to protecting adults, is concerned that in the contemporary hysteria too many innocent adults are being unjustly accused. The polarization among professionals is now so bad that researchers are quickly branded as being on one side or the other, and their work discounted by the opposition.

—*Carol Tavris*

Two months after its founding in March 1992, the FMSF claimed 413 members, all of whom said they were victims of false accusations, most made after their adult daughters had recovered memories in therapy.

Like me, the culture seemed to be running on two tracks, alternately excoriating abusers and false accusers, simultaneously believing and not believing those who said they'd been abused.

Once again the media were mocking and discrediting the feminist researchers, therapists, and activists who'd broken the incest story. The feminists who'd opposed the anti-pornography activists' Puritanism years ago were protesting their sisters' role in the sex-panic now.

The Wall Street Journal
February 22, 1993
"Modern Witch Hunt—Child Abuse Charges"

Child abuse allegations are the third-greatest wave of hysteria the nation has seen, following the Salem witch trials and the McCarthyite persecution of leftists. . . .

The first, the Salem Witch Trials, in 1692, lasted only a few months. Nineteen people were hanged before it became apparent that the accusations were suspect. In the 1950s, at the time of the McCarthy hearings, hysteria over the communist threat resulted in the destruction of many careers.

Our current hysteria, which began in the early 1980s, is by far the worst with regard to the number of lives that have been destroyed and families that have disintegrated.

—Richard Gardner

The New York Times, The Wall Street Journal—I expected disbelief from them. But Mother Jones was my most trusted news source and the only magazine to which I subscribed.

So when I found a story about a case of recovered memory in the January 1993 issue, I assumed that although the writer was a man—what were the editors *thinking?*—he'd be on the right side of the issue. And then I had to stop and wonder what, exactly, that side was, and whom I trusted to speak for it, and what its tenets were.

Mother Jones
January-February 1993
"Doors of Memory"

Most nights, in most U.S. cities, "adult survivors" meet in church basements or community-center conference rooms, hold stuffed animals to their chests, and share newly discovered memories of sexual abuse.

"When someone who claims an expertise in how the mind works convinces a subject that what they imagine equates to a memory, there is almost no memory that you couldn't produce," says University of California sociologist Dr. Richard Ofshe, who has studied methods of influence used by cults.

"You can get people to believe that they led past lives where they fought intergalactic wars. You could arbitrarily make up any event and stand a good chance of creating a memory around it."

"The simple solution is very attractive," says Dr. Richard Gardner, a clinical professor of child psychiatry at Columbia University. "You're thirty-five or forty and your life is all screwed up, and someone offers this very simple solution: 'Ah, I never realized that I was sexually abused. That explains it all!'—it's a simple answer for the therapist as well as the patient."

—Ethan Watters

I was mortified. The one source I trusted had gone over to the dark side.

How could *Mother Jones* have fallen for the FMSF party line? Richard Ofshe, FMSF board member, the mouthpiece for those who refused to believe women and children—quoted as a reliable expert in *Mother Jones*?

I rushed to my computer to write an outraged letter to the editor. Then I thought about how I'd envied Jane her certainty, her horrifying memories, her courage in the face of victimhood. How I'd wished that I deserved the nurturing that Jane's abuse had earned her. How I'd wished there was a one-word explanation for my less admirable traits.

Were Ofshe and Gardner right about me? I asked myself.

Had I created my incest memories, looking for a simple solution?

The New York Times
April 4, 1993

To the Editor:

As the author of "Confabulations: Creating False Memories—Destroying Families," I have spoken to hundreds of parents of adult children across the United States, Canada and England. They all have the same remarkable story: their children accuse them of abuse after decades-delayed discoveries that emerge in therapy from repressed memories.

The acts of cruelty to so-called perpetrators are amazing—angry letters written to all family members, public disclosure, notes passed at weddings, deathbed encounters and lawsuits.

...Data exist that show thousands of families are suffering from the effects of false memory syndrome...The issue merits investigation by unbiased experts, without delay.

—*Eleanor Goldstein*
Boca Raton, Fla.

In its May 17 and May 24 issues, another trusted source, the *New Yorker*, published a two-part story by staff writer Lawrence Wright. "Remembering Satan" detailed the case of Olympia, Washington, sheriff Paul Ingram, whose twenty-two- and eighteen-year-old daughters had accused him of molesting them.

Reading the article, I thought, *If I have to have a molester for a father, I wish at least he loved me enough to admit what he did to me.*

I heard myself and I was incredulous. *I'm envying two women whose father molested them.*

The New Yorker
May 17, 1993
"Remembering Satan"

"Paul, there's a problem," [Ingram's supervisor] Gary Edwards said. He asked if Ingram knew about the charges of sexual molestation that his two daughters . . . had made.

Ingram said that he did; however, he said he could not remember having ever molested his daughters. "If this did happen, we need to take care of it," Ingram said, but he added, "I can't see myself doing this." If he did molest the girls, then "there must be a dark side of me that I don't know about." . . . He requested a lie detector test, so he could "get to the bottom of this."

. . . Several hours into the questioning . . . Ingram now said, "I really believe that the allegations did occur and that I did violate them and probably for a long period of time. I've repressed it."

—*Lawrence Wright*

This is crazy. And I don't want to be crazy anymore.

The American Medical Association released a policy statement on recovered memory.

The AMA considers recovered memories of childhood sexual abuse to be of uncertain authenticity, which should be subject to external verification. The use of recovered memories is fraught with problems of potential misapplication.

The American Psychiatric Association weighed in, too.

There is no uniform "profile" or other method to accurately distinguish those who have sexually abused children from those who have not. . . . It is not known how to distinguish, with complete accuracy, memories based on true events from those derived from other sources.

Memories also can be significantly influenced by a trusted person (e.g., therapist, parent involved in a custody dispute) who suggests abuse as an explanation for symptoms/problems, despite initial lack of memory of such abuse.

Time Magazine
November 29, 1993
"Lies of the Mind"

Suffering from a prolonged bout of depression, Melody Gavigan, 39, a computer specialist from Long Beach, California, checked herself into a local psychiatric hospital.

During five weeks of treatment there . . . she went on to recall being molested by her father when she was only a year old. . . . Gavigan confronted her father with her accusations, severed her relationship with him, moved away and formed an incest survivors' group.

Signing up for a college psychology course, she examined her newfound memories more carefully and concluded that they were false. Now Gavigan has begged her father's forgiveness and filed a lawsuit against the psychiatric hospital for the pain that she and her family suffered.

> Gavigan is just one victim of a troubling psychological phenom-
> enon that is . . . intensifying a backlash against all mental-health
> practitioners: the "recovery"—usually while in therapy—of repressed
> memories of childhood sexual abuse, satanic rituals and other bizarre
> incidents.
>
> Across the U.S. in the past several years, literally thousands of
> people—mostly women in their 20s, 30s and 40s—have been coming
> forward with accusations that they were sexually abused as
> children.
>
> "Recovered-memory therapy will come to be recognized as the
> quackery of the 20th century," predicts Richard Ofshe, a social
> psychologist at the University of California, Berkeley.
>
> —Leon Jaroff and Jeanne McDowell

I found a new book in the Child Abuse section at Cody's Books: *Satanic Panic: The Creation of a Contemporary Legend,* by sociologist Jeffrey Victor.

"Some really bizarre things have been happening in this country," Victor wrote on page 1. "These strange happenings may be omens of one of the biggest secret conspiracies, or one of the biggest hoaxes, in recent history."

Victor offered a list of examples from the past several years:

Two adult daughters brought a suit against their seventy-six-year-old mother . . . charging her with having sexually abused and tortured them in Satanic Cult rituals. The women also accused their mother and the cult of having forced them to kill their own babies born out of rape.

About five hundred people turned out in Rupert, Idaho, to attend a prayer vigil for babies ritually tortured and killed by satanic cults. [The vigil] was organized by local ministers to commemorate the discovery of the mutilated and burned corpse of "baby X" found at a landfill two years before.

"None of these claims are supported by reliable evidence," Victor concluded. "[New] research findings can help us understand the social dynamics of rumor-panics, national scares, and witch hunts [and] enable us to better understand how societies create imaginary deviance and . . . collective fear and persecutions."

Rumor-panics? Witch hunts? *Imaginary deviance and persecutions?*

Reading this filled me with the outrage I'd felt reading Ethan Watters's piece in *Mother Jones.* Yes, I'd been finding Jane's stories of ritual abuse harder and harder to believe. Yes, the number and severity of the preschool abuse cases and daughter-father accusations made me wonder whether some of the claims were overstated—including mine.

But . . . *imaginary deviance?* Tell that to the Rand daughters, Mr. Victor. Despite my own uncertainty, this sudden rash of counterclaims felt more like a backlash than a breakthrough, another round of that good old American hear-no-evil, see-no-evil denial that had come and gone and come again since the country was born.

At the same time, I couldn't help but wonder: How could Jane's story be so similar to the stories of toddlers across the country? And how could the stories of toddlers three thousand miles apart so closely match each other's?

Which brought me back to the question I'd been asking for years now, with no discernable progress toward an answer.

Did he or didn't he?

What's true? What's false?

part three

1994–2009

There are three sides to every story: yours, mine, and the truth.

—*Robert Evans*, The Kid Stays in the Picture

nine

Doubt

How, in just fifteen years, did we go from the
suppression of children's experiences, women's
experiences, such that they were not ever heard—
to a level of cacophony such that children's voices,
women's voices, are once more not, in any
purposeful sense, being heard?

> —*Louise Armstrong*, Rocking the Cradle
> of Sexual Politics: What Happened
> When Women Said Incest, *1994*

Library Journal
January 31, 1994
"Review of *Unchained Memories: True Stories of Traumatic Memories Lost and Found*, by Lenore Terr, M.D."

Much controversy exists about whether or not childhood memories
repressed for many years can be fully retrieved in adulthood without
major distortions (otherwise known as the "false memory" debate).
In this fascinating book, Terr, author of *Too Scared to Cry* . . . argues
that . . . taking a general stand on the truth or falsity of such memories
is a mistake.

—*January Adams, ODSI Research Librarian, Raritan, New Jersey*

The anti-porn movement of the 1970s had spawned an uneasy alliance between anti-rape feminists and family-protection conservatives. Twenty years later, the campaign to save children from the devil—defined by feminists as incestuous fathers, by family-values right-wingers as satanist preschool teachers—was making strange bedfellows of the two camps again.

What was going on *out there* was also going on *in here*. Like the rest of the world, it seemed, I was fighting the incest war from both sides.

The more I disbelieved myself, the more I disbelieved Jane. One minute I wanted to leave her or hook her up to a polygraph machine while she slept. The next I was flooded with love for her, and pity. After all she'd been through, she was stuck with an uncompassionate, unfeminist bitch: me.

Our relationship had never exactly been a pillar of stability, and my flip-flopping wasn't helping. So as Jane and I dropped the kids at their dad's and headed off to the mountains for a much-needed Christmas break, I was hoping it wouldn't be the psychotic kind. *Please*, I prayed as I steered my Honda wagon north on Highway 101, *just let us get through the week without a breakdown or a breakup.*

On the outskirts of Cloverdale, we saw signs of activity at the side of the highway, a dusty pullout full of haphazardly parked cars. "Oh, my God," Jane said. "This is where they found Polly Klaas."

She didn't have to remind me who Polly was. I slowed the car.

A few weeks earlier, the twelve-year-old had been kidnapped from her bed in bucolic, suburban Petaluma, then raped and murdered. When her killer was caught, he'd led the police to the spot where he'd buried her: here.

I parked between two mud-spattered pickup trucks, and Jane and I walked toward the crowd that was gathered at a homemade altar—not holding hands, bodies tensed against the homophobic hostilities we often encountered outside the gay-friendly Bay Area bubble. At the edge of a field, a blown-up photo of Polly smiled from an easel, surrounded by the flotsam and jetsam of public grief: notes scribbled on binder paper in children's handwriting, teddy bears with their fuzzy paws wrapped around red felt hearts, wrinkled helium balloons floating at half-mast, vases stuffed with cheap plastic flowers and extravagant wildflower bouquets.

Women and their daughters—there wasn't a single man here, not one boy—kneeled in the dirt to add a teddy bear or a flower and then bowed their heads and cried.

As Jane began to weep, I was flooded with the truth of the moment. There was nothing debatable about what had happened to Polly on this piece of scrabbled ground. My chronic ambivalence was swept out on a wave of crystalline clarity: the unequivocal outrage that had started me caring and writing about incest more than a decade ago.

I had a choice to make. I could go on duking it out with my disbelief and my resentments until my head—and my relationship with Jane—exploded. Or I could turn my attention to what really mattered, to the simple clarity of knowing what needed to be done and doing it.

Three months later, I started writing a book called *Notes from an Incomplete Revolution: Real Life Since Feminism*. I dedicated the book to Jane and all the girls and women like Jane. Finally, I knew what was true, and I knew what to do about it.

I didn't need to look far for a place to start. I'd been following the trial of Napa, California, wine executive Gary Ramona. Ramona was suing the therapists who'd treated his daughter, Holly, before she accused him of raping and sodomizing her. And the Napa County Courthouse, at which the trial was being held, was only an hour's drive from my house.

The Independent (U.K.)
April 22, 1994
"Did Someone Play Tricks on Holly's Mind?"

Holly Ramona, 23, tells a court that her father, a wealthy Californian wine executive, raped her as a child. But it is not Daddy who is in the dock: it's Holly's therapist and psychiatrist. Did they plant the memory in her head? America awaits the verdict.

"I can remember my father was on top of me," [Holly Ramona] told the packed courtroom. "He was heavy. I could feel his skin and I could smell him. I remember wanting him to go away. . . ."

[Ramona's] wife divorced him, his friends ostracised him, his two other daughters severed relations, and Holly Ramona filed a lawsuit. Now, vigorously protesting his innocence, he has launched a counter-attack. . . . Mr. Ramona is seeking to persuade a jury that he should be paid more than dollars 8m damages by his daughter's therapist and a psychiatrist because, he says, they planted false memories in her mind.

The trial . . . raises the troubled question of whether people genuinely suppress recollections of sexual abuse during childhood. Do they "forget" experiences that are too horrible to confront? Or are some unwittingly coerced by over-zealous therapists into inventing them?

—Phil Reeves

In the courthouse lobby, I approached a bored-looking guard. "Excuse me. I'm looking for the trial of—"

"Second floor," he said.

A crowd milled in the hallway outside the courtroom. Three separate crowds, actually: a handful of reporters with bulging shoulder bags and narrow notepads; a dozen well-coiffed, middle-aged women in linen and tweed and posh leather pumps; and fifteen men in suits and ties accompanied by the same number of boys, each dressed the same way. Why, I wondered, would anyone bring a child to this trial?

A guard opened the courtroom doors. I followed the others inside. The reporters headed purposefully to the seats on the right side of the room. The men in suits and the children sat there, too. The women arranged themselves on the left.

Normally I'd sit with the reporters. But it was clear that the two sides of the courtroom reflected the two sides in this trial, which is to say, the two sides in the war that had spawned it. I wanted to sit with the people on my side.

A man slid into the seat next to mine. My body tensed. Which side was he on?

"John," he said, extending his hand. "I think what that man did to his daughter is sick beyond belief. Don't you?"

The right side. I nodded and shook his hand.

"I've been coming to this trial every day for six weeks." John pointed to the two women in front of us. "That's Holly's mom, Stephanie Ramona. And Holly's grandma. Nice ladies."

He ducked his head toward the defense table. "Holly's therapist. And her psychiatrist." He gazed at a beautiful young woman with flawless skin and a thin black velvet headband through her thick, brown, shoulder-length hair. "That's Holly."

John scowled at the men in the seats across the aisle. "And those are the fathers," he said. "They're from the Sacramento chapter of the False Memory Syndrome Foundation. There's a busload of them here every day. And every day they bring all those kids with them.

"They'll tell anyone who'll listen their stories. And their stories are all the same. They say their daughters ruined their lives with their false incest accusations. And that guy . . ." John pointed to the prosecution table. "That's the sleaze ball. Gary Ramona."

I stared at Ramona's back: his tailored olive-green suit, his thinning brown hair strategically arranged on his balding head.

From here he looked a lot like my father. My father six years ago, the last time I'd seen or spoken to him.

For the next three hours, Gary Ramona's attorney interrogated his daughter's therapists. What made them decide to administer the "truth serum" (sodium amytal) that had produced Holly's memories—"flashbacks," Gary Ramona's lawyer sneered—of a dozen incidents of abuse and rape between the ages of five and eight?

Were they actually flashbacks, or just "senseless, short flashes that occur very commonly to people with bulimia"?

What did Holly's psychiatrist mean, exactly, when he wrote in his notes that the sodium amytal helped Holly "remember specific details of sexual molestation"?

The elder Ramona's attorney called expert witnesses, one of whom testified that sodium amytal is "not useful in ascertaining 'truth.' . . . The patient becomes sensitive and receptive to suggestions due to the context and to the comments of the interviewers."

Under his questioning, recovered-memory expert Dr. Lenore Terr admitted that Holly's memory of being forced to perform oral sex on the family dog was "dubious."

Clearly fearing the worst, Holly's distraught therapist warned that a decision in favor of Gary Ramona would put survivors "in the position of 'I can't really tell anyone what happened to me' and cast 'a blow for anyone with memories of sexual abuse.'"

During the morning break, I wandered down the hall to the water fountain. The prepubescent boy ahead of me took a drink, turned, and slipped on the slick linoleum in the courthouse hallway. "Careful, son," one of the FMSF men called to him. "You'll get hurt. Then the next thing we know, you'll be having *flashbacks* and *recovered memories!*"

"Oh!" the boy exclaimed melodramatically. "I'm having a flashback!" He and the men broke into laughter. I slunk back inside.

At the lunch break I stayed in my seat, typing my notes into my laptop computer. A shadow fell across my screen. I looked up into the grinning face of Gary Ramona. I shuddered involuntarily.

"Is that a Macintosh?" he asked. I was suddenly aware of the V-necked blouse I was wearing, of the view it afforded as he stared down at me. I sat up straight.

"Is that the mouse?" he asked, reaching toward the computer in my lap. I jumped to my feet and glared at him.

"Are you a reporter?" Ramona asked, undaunted. "Here for a newspaper? A magazine?"

"I'm here for myself," I said, and I grabbed my stuff and rushed out of the courtroom. In the bathroom I splashed water on my flushed face, *flashing back* on the symptoms that Holly's lawyer had cited as proof of her client's abuse. Her depression and bulimia. Her recurring nightmares of snakes crawling up her vagina. Her refusal to have a gynecological exam. Her aversion to whole bananas, melted cheese, and mayonnaise, which reminded her of being forced to perform oral sex on her father.

Bulimia and depression are symptoms of child sexual abuse, I reminded myself.

Not always. How many upper-middle-class girls who weren't abused get depressed and bulimic in college, as Holly Ramona did?

But what could make a little girl dream about snakes crawling up her vagina? If Holly hadn't been raped as a child, why would she have refused a pelvic exam?

When I had my first pelvic exam at age twelve, the doctor asked why my hymen was torn: number eleven on my list of incest symptoms.

After lunch Holly took the stand.

"I was always afraid of him," she testified. "He gave me the creeps. If he came into the room, I would leave. I couldn't understand why I was having these feelings. I felt guilty for feeling so much dislike for him."

Holly talked about her first incest memory: an image of her father's hand on her stomach. And then there were more. "I couldn't control them," she said. "Sometimes they would come back when I was going to bed. Sometimes they would come when I was driving. I felt like I was going crazy."

"If your father's innocent," the lawyer asked, "why would he be fighting you in court?"

"He wants control," Holly answered. "And he's getting exactly what he wants."

"Are you absolutely certain that your father raped you?" the attorney asked.

"I'm absolutely certain," she said. "If I wasn't, I wouldn't be here."

Gary Ramona's lawyer called wine mogul Robert Mondavi as a character witness. As he was being sworn in, the FMSF fathers elbowed each other, nodding and smiling. The reporters snapped to attention, pens poised.

Mondavi talked about what a wonderful person Gary Ramona was. He'd never doubted Gary's innocence, he said. He just couldn't understand why Holly was making these accusations. "They were just a beautiful family," Mondavi said. "I saw a lot of affection."

The lawyer called Holly back to the stand and handed her a greeting card. "Is this the Father's Day card you sent you father five years ago?" he asked.

Holly stared down at the card, grimacing. Then she nodded.

"Please read it aloud," the lawyer instructed her.

"You are the Dad who has got it all," she recited, her voice wavering for the first time.

"And how did you sign your card to your father?"

Holly looked at her father and then back at the card in her hand. "Your great love, Holly," she said, and burst into tears. In front of me, Holly's mother slumped in her seat.

I want to be my father's great love again, I thought.

I needed help, and Catherine was gone, and going back to Ruth felt like . . . going back. A survivor friend recommended a Rosen bodyworker who was also a licensed therapist.

"Incest accusations don't arise in healthy families," Miranda said when I told her why I was there.

"So you think my father did it," I said.

"I have no way to know that."

"But you'll help me figure it out," I pressed her.

"I can help you figure out what's true for you," Miranda answered. "I can help you focus on what you do know, instead of focusing on what you don't."

I briefly considered asking for a refund. Disappointed and dubious, I climbed onto her table.

Imagine my surprise. Swaddled in warm flannel blankets, stripped of my sharpest self-defense weapon, words, I felt stirrings of something strange and good.

Miranda's certain, confident touch made me feel cared for and held and believed. Deprived of my words, in that silence, I began to believe myself.

I left Miranda's office with an appointment for the following week. The good news was, Miranda had helped me hear my own voice. The bad news was, my voice was telling me things about my relationship with Jane, things about my accusation against my father that I didn't want to hear.

My editor at *Parenting* magazine asked me to write a "provocative" opinion piece for the magazine's Up in Arms column. The subject: the child sexual abuse charges against pop star Michael Jackson. She'd read my incest exposés, so I knew which side of the controversy she wanted me to take.

As a little boy, Charlie revered Michael Jackson. His room was a veritable museum of Michael memorabilia. Charlie drew his hero's likeness tirelessly, practiced his moonwalk endlessly, dressed as Michael every Halloween for several years running. He refused to remove his fingerless glittery glove, which I took to peeling off his hand while he slept so I could wash the filthy thing. Still, there was no question in my mind that the accusations against Michael Jackson were true.

In the four-month lag time between my writing of the piece and its publication, Jackson settled with the accusing family for $22 million. The civil case was dropped for lack of evidence.

By the time my essay appeared, I was no longer sure of Michael Jackson's guilt. Maybe he had done it. Or maybe his prosecution was one more case of the "rumor-panics, national scares, and witch hunts" that Jeffrey Victor and the FMSF—and a tiny little voice in me—believed it to be.

Jane took a week off work and flew back East to research her memories.

Now *she* was the investigative reporter, spending days poring over microfiche in the local public library, looking for old newspaper stories about her father, about babies who'd gone missing, about local satanic cults. She found no sign of any of it. "Maybe there's been a cover-up," she told me when she called. Her father had been a powerful man in their town. He could have made the evidence disappear.

She drove to the woods near her childhood home and searched for evidence of a fire pit or a grave, for remnants of the rituals she'd seen in her sessions and her dreams. On her last night there she called me, sounding triumphant: she'd found a circle of charred rocks.

This is insane, I thought. "Maybe someone built a campfire in those woods sometime in the past twenty years," I said.

Silence crackled between us. "If you'd seen the way my body reacted when I was standing in that spot," Jane said, "you couldn't possibly say that. I was shaking so hard, I nearly passed out."

"I believe you," I lied.

> ## The New York Times
> ### May 14, 1994
> ### "Father Who Fought 'Memory Therapy' Wins Damage Suit"
>
> In a groundbreaking legal verdict, a Napa County jury awarded $500,000 today to a father who had accused psychotherapists of conning his adult daughter into remembering childhood incidents of incest that he said had never occurred.
>
> Mental health experts said that as a result of today's jury verdict the relatively new technique of recovered-memory therapy, as well as those who practice it, would at least come under closer scrutiny.
>
> In a statement issued immediately after the verdict was announced, Mr. Ramona said: "The jury saw what I've always known: that Holly's supposed memories are the result of the defendants' drugs and quackery, not anything I did."
>
> —B. Drummond Ayres Jr.

The newspapers and magazines that had once published my incest articles, the talk shows that once lauded the courage of incest survivors still bristled with exposés—but the script had flipped. The emergency issue was no longer child sexual abuse. The new crisis was about families torn apart by false claims of child sexual abuse.

In my mailbox, *Esquire*, March 1994: "The Lost Daughter: How One American Family Got Caught Up in Today's Witches' Brew of Sexual Abuse, the Sybil Syndrome, and the Perverse Ministrations of the Therapy Police."

In my morning paper, the *San Francisco Chronicle*, for several days running: a Doonesbury strip featuring a therapist and his hypnotized client.

"You're in your own bed . . . someone quietly steps from the shadows. Who is it?" the therapist asks.

"It's Lyndon Johnson," the client answers.

"No, no, it's your father," insists the therapist.

Also in the *Chronicle*, a column by the liberal Jon Carroll: "Are You Nuts, or Just in Denial?"

> In the vast world of pop-psych repressed-memory handbooks, almost anything can be a sign of childhood sexual abuse.
>
> You may have one or more of these symptoms, and yet you sincerely believe that you were not abused as a child. Clearly, you are in denial.
>
> Next week: breathing, a key sign of incest.

Like many American phenomena, "the memory war," as the controversy was now known, was slower to reach the middle of the country. The June 1994 issue of Mom-and-apple-pie *Redbook* carried a story called "Blame It on the Devil." The article reported on a study by trauma expert Dr. Colin Ross.

> Seventy percent of Americans believe that at least some people who claim that they were abused by satanic cults as children but repressed the memories for years are telling the truth. . . .
>
> . . . Thirty-two percent say that the FBI and the police ignore evidence because they don't want to admit the cults exist.

In the January 17, 1994, issue of the False Memory Syndrome Foundation newsletter, the organization claimed a membership of 6,007 falsely accused families—up from 243 two years before.

One Thursday night, I came home from the gym and found a group of strangers in my living room, standing in a circle, holding hands with their eyes closed.

I froze in the doorway. These strangers were *strange*: strangely dressed, behaving strangely. They were so engrossed in what they were doing—*what the hell* were *they doing?*—that they didn't notice me.

It's some kind of cult, I thought, and then I saw that Jane was one of them, and I remembered. Two weeks ago she'd joined a support group for survivors of satanic ritual abuse. She'd told me this morning—*I must have repressed it*—that they'd be meeting here tonight.

I backed out of the room, tiptoed upstairs, closed myself into my bedroom, and sat, dazed, on the edge of my bed. How had my life gotten this crazy?

Be compassionate, I scolded myself. *Be Jane's hero.*

When she came to bed an hour later, I chained myself to that thought—*be Jane's hero*. While she told me about the meeting, I listened actively, doing my best imitation of a trusting and trustworthy person.

Several of the women, Jane said, were "multiples" with "MPD": Multiple Personality Disorder. They'd "split" into "alternate personalities" to cope with the trauma of their abuse.

When a multiple was "triggered" by something that reminded her of the abuse—the sight of a naked man in a movie, an evocative smell, or (uh-oh) a harsh word from her lover—she switched from her "primary personality" to one of her "alters." *Translation: when Jane started splitting into her alters, it would be my fault.*

I took a deep breath. Ever attuned to my ambivalence, Jane sat up and squinted at me.

"You read *Sybil*, didn't you?" she said in that voice that meant *You don't believe me*. "She was horribly abused as a child, and she ended up with sixteen personalities."

I can barely live with one of you, I thought. *I definitely can't handle sixteen.* "Everyone knows that book was a hoax," I blurted. So much for my impersonation of a decent human being.

Jane glared at me. "If you'd been through what *we've* been through . . . ," she said.

Jane's "we," I realized, wasn't the two of us anymore. Now "we" consisted of her sister survivors of satanic ritual abuse. Not a club that would have me as a member. And not a club I wanted to join.

"You're right," I said. "What you've been through is hard for me to understand."

Jane hurled herself out of my bed and stomped upstairs to her own. The sound of her sobbing drifted down the stairs. *Be her hero,* I told myself. *Go to her. Comfort her. Save her.*

I was a leaky vessel, empty. I didn't even know how to save myself.

Publisher's Weekly
October 1994
"Review of *Making Monsters: False Memories, Psychotherapy, and Sexual Hysteria,* by Richard Ofshe and Ethan Watters"

This is the most thoroughgoing and powerful critique to date of the use of recovered memories in psychotherapy.

Many retrieved memories of childhood sexual abuse, the authors argue, are fabrications generated in a coercive, highly charged atmosphere using questionable therapeutic techniques such as hypnosis, dream analysis, artwork and the constant revisiting and rewriting of vague early memories.

Ofshe, a social psychology professor at UC Berkeley and a Pulitzer-winning reporter, and freelance writer Watters extend their analysis to include alleged sufferers of multiple-personality disorder and people who claim to have been abused or tortured by satanic cults that engage in sacrificial murder and rape.

. . . This report is certain to escalate a heated public debate.

—*Reed Business Information*

"I need to talk to you, Mer," my sister-in-law, Susie, said.

The kids were watching TV in my room, so I took the phone into theirs and closed the door.

"Your dad and Gloria want to take Emmy and Zach to Europe," Susie said.

My first thought was of my kids: how envious they'd be, and how sad. They'd never been to Europe, and given my freelance finances, they were unlikely to get there anytime soon.

"For a month," Susie added. "Doug and I discussed it, and we decided to leave it up to you. Should we let them go?"

Six years ago when my accusation was new, Doug and Susie had asked if they should leave their kids alone with my dad. I'd said they shouldn't, and they'd taken my advice. I'd been ambivalent then. I was less ambivalent now.

"Let them go," I said.

"But . . . if there's even a chance he'd do to Emmy what he did to you . . ."

"He won't," I said.

After a long silence, Susie asked, "Do you still think your father molested you?"

"I don't know," I answered.

I remembered what a relief it had been, declaring myself an incest survivor. It was even more of a relief to admit that I didn't know whether I was one.

Why had I thought *not knowing* made me weak? I felt strong now, the way I did on Miranda's table.

"Does your mother know that you changed your . . ." Susie hesitated. "That you're not sure it's true?"

"No." Since I'd made my accusation, the fragile filament that connected my mother and me had frayed even more.

"What are you going to do about your dad?" Susie asked.

"I don't know," I said again.

PBS ran a series about the memory war called *Divided Memories*. As a feminist I was infuriated by the series' assumption that all recovered memories were false memories.

As a journalist I was "following the money," and I wasn't alone. In her 1994 book *Rocking the Cradle of Sexual Politics,* Louise Armstrong wrote, "Between 1975 and 1990 the number of American psychiatrists and other mental health professionals increased from 72,000 to 198,000. This explosion roughly parallels the rise of the issue of incest, and thousands (if not in fact tens of thousands) of these professionals now put themselves forward as a resource specifically for incest-related disorders."

As a daughter I watched the interviews with "retractors"— women who'd recovered memories of childhood abuse and later realized that those memories were false—and wondered if "retractor" would be the next label I wore.

Time Magazine
May 22, 1995
"Chronicle of a Witch Hunt"

During the 1980s, hysteria lived in comfortable homes with jungle gyms out back and family vans parked in front. Spurred by public outrage, prosecutors charged staff members with horrific crimes . . . though their reputations were irrevocably damaged, most of the defendants ultimately went free.

Among them were Virginia McMartin, her daughter Peggy and two grown grandchildren. . . . The case ended in 1990 with no convictions on any of the 65 criminal counts.

Now the family's seven-year legal ordeal is the subject of *Indictment: The McMartin Trial,* a gripping—though excessively pious— TV movie. . . . The biggest villains in the movie are the media. From talk-show hosts to newspaper reporters, the media avidly portrayed the McMartins as torturers.

Indictment has already raised an outcry among children's advocacy groups. In a press release, the American Professional Society

}

The cordless phone in my pocket rang while I was in the garden, patting tender lettuce seedlings into moist, wormy black soil.

"Mer," my brother said. His voice was pinched, as if he were squeezing it through a lump in his throat.

I sat back on my heels. "What's wrong?"

"It's Dad. He had a heart attack."

I clenched the phone. "Is he—?"

"It wasn't a bad one. He'll be okay."

Not dead. Thank God, he's not dead.

"I'm coming." I jumped to my feet. "Where is he?"

After a long silence Doug said, "He's in the hospital."

I didn't have to ask why he wasn't telling me where my father was. And I didn't have to ask why my brother—or my father or stepmother or father's doctors, whoever had made the decision—didn't want me there with him.

"Give him my love," I said.

This has to stop, I thought. *I have to stop this while there's still time.*

ten

Deprogramming

I want to announce publicly that as a firm believer
in the "Believe the Children" movement of the
1980s that started with the McMartin trials in
California, now I am convinced that I was terribly
wrong. . . .

. . . And many innocent people were convicted
and went to prison as a result. . . .

. . . And I am equally positive [that the]
"Repressed Memory Therapy Movement" is also a
bunch of crap.
—*Geraldo Rivera, CNBC, December 12, 1995,*
as quoted in Mary de Young, The Day Care
Ritual Abuse Moral Panic, *2004*

"I want to make up with my father," I said.

I was lying on Miranda's table, face up, eyes closed, her hands
cradling my head from behind.

"Your body agrees with that," Miranda murmured in that
Rosen bodywork voice of hers.

That room, that table, had been my sanctuary since the day
I'd walked into it a year before. But when Miranda used Rosen
jargon, I felt as though I'd joined another cult with another weird
language, like co-counseling, like incest survivorhood. Which

prompted me to make nervous jokes to prove—to myself, to Miranda—that I was still capable of independent thought. Which shut the whole process down. Which kind of defeated the purpose. Not to mention the wasted eighty-five bucks.

No money wasted today; my body *did* agree with that. But not so my mind, which played out the consequences of reconciling with my father and set off sirens and flashing lights. Inviting my father back into my life would jeopardize everything that had kept me going for the past several years: my righteous anger, my victimhood, my citizenship in Incest Nation, my friendships, maybe even my relationship with my lover.

"My body's been wrong before," I said. "What do *you* think?"

I heard the smile in Miranda's voice. "I think you know I won't answer that question."

I sighed. "A girl can dream."

Miranda moved her hands to my shoulder blades, probing, kneading, melting my resistance. "I'm afraid I'll lose everything if I forgive him," I said.

Miranda's fingers dug deeper. "What just got put away?" she asked. Again with the Rosen-speak. Again she was right.

"I'm not sure I have anything to forgive him for," I said. "Maybe I'm the one who should beg for forgiveness."

"Does it matter?"

How could she ask me that? "That's *all* that matters."

"It seems to me that if you and your dad want to be in each other's lives," Miranda said, "you'll need to forgive each other."

I trusted Miranda as much as I'd ever trusted anyone: pathetic, but true. So as she walked around the table and took my feet in her hands, holding them as tenderly as she would a newborn baby, I forced myself to consider her point of view.

Maybe this story has no good guy and no bad guy.

I imagined telling Jane that I was going to start seeing my father again. She'd ask the obvious question. *So you don't think he abused you?* And then our relationship would be even more strained than it was.

Apparently I'd been visualizing out loud. "What's more important?" Miranda said—with incredible patience, considering. "What Jane thinks? Or what you think?"

Her fingers, insisting.

"I'm not sure," I answered, my new favorite thing to say.

"Can you tell Jane what's true for you?"

"I don't *know* what's true for me."

"Can you tell her *that?*" Miranda pressed me, literally and figuratively.

"I don't know," I said.

> ### Hillsborough County Superior Court, State of New Hampshire
> #### May 23, 1995
> #### "Ruling of Judge William J. Groff in *State of New Hampshire v. Joel Hungerford* and *State of New Hampshire v. John Morahan*"
>
> . . . the phenomenon of memory repression, and the process of therapy used in these cases to recover the memories, have not gained general acceptance in the field of psychology, and are not scientifically reliable.

That expression, "Serious as a heart attack"—I got it now.

Whatever my accusation had been when I'd made it—a statement of truth, a statement of truth as I'd seen it at the time, a statement of solidarity with wounded girls and women everywhere, a crowbar I used to pry my father out of my head—it was something else now.

It was the family I'd promised my children, denied. It was my integrity, compromised. And now, in the aftermath of my father's heart attack, it was, quite possibly, a matter of life and death.

As the memory war escalated, so did the animosity between those who still "believed the children" and those who attributed the skyrocketing rate of child sexual abuse to mass hysteria.

By acknowledging their own excesses, the child-believers risked reversing the hard-earned gains they'd made. Those "on the other side," as represented by the FMSF, were desperate to stop what they saw as the mass prosecution of innocents.

I'd never been much of a moderate, and I wasn't comfortable where I found myself: perched dead center, an uneasy bird on the wire.

So I jumped. I took *The Courage to Heal* off my bedside reading pile, where it had lived for seven years, and moved it to the living room bookshelf, out of sight if not out of mind. On my next trip to Cody's, I found a different kind of incest book in the Child Abuse section—a shelf full of books that disputed the existence of recovered memory.

Remembering Satan, by Lawrence Wright, based on his *New Yorker* article about the Washington sheriff who'd pled guilty to ritually abusing his daughters, and later retracted his confession

Return of the Furies, by Ralph Underwager, dedicated to FMSF founders Pam and Peter Freyd

Victims of Memory, by FMSF member Mark Pendergrast, blurbed by Elizabeth Loftus

Suggestions of Abuse, by Michael Yapko, blurbed by Elizabeth Loftus

Lost Daughters, by Reinder Van Til, blurbed by Elizabeth Loftus

Satan's Silence, by Debbie Nathan and Michael Snedeker, blurbed by Elizabeth Loftus

The Myth of Repressed Memory, by Elizabeth Loftus

It appeared that Geraldo Rivera had been reading some of these "backlash books" too.

On June 29, 1995, four years after his last show about satanic ritual abuse and eight years after his first, Geraldo hosted another one called "The Devil's Innocents: Juvenile Victims of Satanic Abuse."

"Unsubstantiated charges have been made," Geraldo acknowledged, and then added, "It is also painfully clear, however, that stripped of the exaggeration and stripped of the rhetoric, there are many people out there in our country today committing terrible crimes in Satan's name. . . .

"Estimates are that there are over one million satanists in this country. . . . The odds are that this is happening in your town."

One of Rivera's call-in guests was Jeffrey Victor, author of the 1993 book *Satanic Panic: The Creation of a Contemporary Legend*. As audience members booed, Victor blamed the satanic ritual abuse panic on false memories, misinformation, lies, and media hype. He accused Rivera of contributing to the hysteria "in order to entertain the audience."

Rivera retorted that Victor was unwilling to face reality. Their argument ended in a stand-off.

Unsubstantiated charges have been made.

"My father's birthday is in two weeks," I told Miranda. "I'm thinking of sending him a card."

I'd been doing talk therapy instead of bodywork with Miranda lately, so I was sitting on her nubby white cotton couch instead of lying on her table. She was facing me in her baby-poop-brown leather chair.

"Will you be able to handle the fallout?" Miranda asked.

"What fallout?" I wanted her to spell it out; that's why I paid her the big bucks.

Miranda ticked off the possibilities on her fingers. "He could call you, which means you'd talk to him for the first time in seven years. He could *not* call you, which could bring up your old feelings of disappointment and rejection . . ."

"You think I shouldn't do it."

Miranda rolled her eyes at me theatrically.

"I know, I know. It's about what I think," I said. "But can you just tell me—?"

She shot me a meaningful look.

I took a deep breath and reached inside for my own goddamn truth. "Whatever happens," I said, "I'll handle it."

"Whatever happens," Miranda echoed, "I'll be here to help you handle it."

None of the greeting cards in Walgreens' "Happy Birthday Dad" rack seemed quite right.

"Happy Birthday to the World's Greatest Dad"? Might strike a false note.

"You Made Me the Person You Hoped I Would Be"? Was that praise or an accusation?

The best piece of advice my father had ever given me was "Never lose your sense of humor, no matter what." "No matter what" seemed to cover a situation like this. So I moved my search to the humor section.

"Happy Birthday, Dad. Without You I'd Be Nothing." Technically true, but not exactly the message I wanted to convey.

The pop-up golf-club birthday card? My dad had never played golf in his life—or hadn't, last I knew. The cute dad mowing the lawn? I didn't think my nature-phobic father had ever set foot on a lawn, let alone mowed one.

Staring at the endless rows of funny cards and heartfelt cards and cards for Spanish speakers and Christians and African Americans, I decided that Hallmark needed a category for people like me, a significant and highly motivated market.

"Happy Birthday, Dad. I'm sorry I falsely accused you of molesting me."

"I wish you hadn't molested me, Dad, but happy birthday anyway."

"Happy Birthday, Dad. I'm not sure whether you molested me or not, but let's get together and talk about it."

Finally I chose the most innocuous card I could find— "Thinking of You, Dad, on Your Special Day"—a card I never would have picked under normal circumstances, a card my father would recognize for exactly what it was: an attempt to tiptoe over the minefield I'd planted between us. But what could I write on it that was both nonexplosive and true?

I used to complain about the "cold, impersonal" Hallmark birthday cards my father sent me year after year, each inscribed the same way. "Dear Meredith," above the imprinted message; "Love, Dad" beneath it.

Now I saw the method in my father's madness. "Dear Dad," I wrote above the imprinted message. "Love, Meredith," I wrote below.

Before I could change my mind, I walked to the post office and dropped the card into the box. Instantly I felt lighter.

"Where were you?" Jane asked when I got home.

"Errands," I said, not quite the truth, not quite a lie.

A few evenings later, my phone rang while I was washing the dinner dishes. "Hello, Meredith," my father said, in his this-is-serious voice.

My belly clenched as if I were hearing a long-lost lover's voice on the phone.

"Hi, Dad," I choked out.

"Thanks for the birthday card," my father said.

And then the strangest thing happened. I floated up to the ceiling. I floated up to the ceiling, and I looked down and saw myself on Miranda's table, telling her about this phone call from my father.

Miranda was saying, "Floating to the ceiling: that's what little girls do when they're being molested."

"I was washing the dishes and my knees literally buckled," I was telling Miranda. "I had to sit down."

I sat down. "You're welcome," I said to my father.

Such stiff formality between my father and me: the two least polite people on the planet. He was still on one side of the mine-field. I was still on the other.

I wanted to say, *Did you do it, Dad?*

I wanted to say, *I'm sorry, Dad.*

"Can I assume that you're over your . . . foolishness now?" my father asked.

I wanted to say yes. I wanted to say no. I wanted to be a grown woman, the one who lay on Miranda's table knowing herself, knowing her truth.

But in that moment, talking to my father after seven years of not talking to my father, that was not who I was and that was not what I could do. I was the same insecure little girl I'd always been with my dad.

I hated myself for that. I hated my father for that. I hated Miranda for knowing this was what would happen if I talked to him.

"I just wanted to wish you a happy birthday," I said, my voice quavering.

"Are you going to answer my question?" my father said.

That anger of his. "I'm doing the best I can," I said.

"Call me when you can do better," my father snapped, and hung up the phone.

"I spoke to my father today," I told Jane over dinner.

She gaped at me. "He called you?"

I nodded.

"What did *he* want?" she asked, in that hostile voice we always used to talk about our perpetrators.

"I sent him a card," I confessed. "For his birthday."

"Why didn't you tell me?" she asked.

Because if I tell you that I don't believe my own incest story anymore, I'll have to tell you that I don't believe your incest story, either. "We've been fighting so much. I didn't want to fight about that, too," I said, a half-truth, otherwise known as a lie.

That sick feeling was with me all the time now, the same feeling I'd had when Robert and I were trying, trying, trying and failing to be happy together.

I couldn't stand the thought of putting Matthew and Charlie through another divorce. And I couldn't stand the thought of abandoning Jane when she was in so much pain.

So I went on imitating the kind, trusting, trustworthy person I wished I actually were: listening to Jane with imitation empathy; holding her with imitation compassion; reassuring her with imitation kindness when she came home from her therapy sessions and her survivors' support groups, when she woke up screaming in the night.

I did love Jane. I loved her desperately, but . . .

But.

I couldn't say what was true.

I couldn't say, "I know our bond is built on suffering, but I don't want to suffer anymore."

I couldn't say, "If you weren't spending all your money on therapy, we could remodel the kitchen."

I couldn't say, "If it takes this much couple's counseling to keep us together, maybe we shouldn't be a couple."

Most of all I couldn't say, "I don't believe that those horrific things really happened to you."

The New York Times
December 19, 1995
"Virginia McMartin Dies at 88; Figure in Case on Child Abuse"

Virginia McMartin, who founded a preschool that became the center of the longest and most expensive criminal case in American history, died on Sunday.

... Charges against Mrs. McMartin, Peggy Ann Buckey and the teachers were dropped in 1986 for lack of evidence.... Mr. Buckey spent five years in prison before raising bail to obtain his freedom, and his mother was behind bars for two years.

The school is no longer in operation.

—David Stout

Journal entry, April 22, 1996

It isn't the thought of the relationship ending that's the worst. The very worst is the thought of living in this purgatory with no end in sight . . .

In therapy today I cried and asked Miranda, "What's happening to me?" The answer I heard in my head was, "You're opening your heart. All your life you've been waiting to be held and loved by a parent. Jane came along and awakened that hope. Now in giving that (and maybe her) up, that hope is lost."

Here we go again, I thought as yet another therapist ushered Jane and me into her office and we assumed our positions at opposite ends of yet another nubby white cotton couch and Jane started explaining our issues one more time.

"I'm a survivor of satanic ritual abuse," she began.

I can't do this anymore, I thought.

"Maybe you're so unhappy because you're spending so much time and money on your own suffering," I blurted. "Maybe you'd feel better if you volunteered at a soup kitchen instead."

The therapist glared at me as if I'd just set the flag of Incest Nation on fire. And maybe I had.

"You don't believe me," Jane said. "You think I'm making the whole thing up."

I considered this for a moment. "Not the whole thing," I said.

God, it felt good to tell the truth. Good, and terrifying.

"Finally you admit it." Jane's blue eyes went gunmetal grey. "How long have you been pretending to believe me?"

The therapist held her hand up, a traffic cop late to the crash. "Let's slow this down a bit," she said.

But Jane was already off the couch and on her way out of the room.

When I got home, Jane wasn't there. When I woke up in the morning, she wasn't there.

Months before, when the end with Jane was beginning, I'd signed up for a meditation retreat on a farm an hour north of Oakland. It didn't seem like the best survival strategy to sit at home waiting for Jane to come home. So I packed my Thich Nhat Hanh tapes and my Pema Chodron books and went.

On day two I overdosed on something—wheat grass juice, the unrelenting heat, Echinacea, grief. I drove myself back to Oakland, stopping a few times to vomit by the side of the road. I opened the front door of our house and stumbled inside, calling out for Jane.

My voice echoed strangely against the walls. I wandered from one room to the next and finally realized why. Jane was gone. So was everything she owned before what was hers became ours. And now, apparently, was hers again.

Her mother's cutting board, gone from the kitchen counter.

Her rocking chair, scuffmarks on the living room floor.

I climbed the steps to the attic. Dust bunnies blew across the floor, tumbleweeds in a deserted Western-movie town. Her bed was gone, her dressers, her clothes. Her collections of incest books and lesbian anthologies and the gay-parenting book we'd written together. Her photos of me. Of the kids. Of the four of us.

I stumbled back downstairs and stretched out on the couch we'd bought together. Jane had never liked it. Neither had I. We'd grown accustomed to buying things that neither of us liked, compromising because we never loved the same things.

I called my ex-husband and asked if he could keep the kids for an extra day or two. "I'm sick," I told him, a bit of the truth, a bit of a lie.

I couldn't stop crying, so Heidi drove me to Miranda's office for an emergency session.

"You felt too guilty to leave her," Heidi said, her left hand on the steering wheel, her right hand clutching mine. "She spared you that."

"Leaving you was the kindest thing Jane ever did for you," Miranda said, leaning forward in her leather chair. "Now you're free."

I didn't feel free. I knew they were right, and I wanted to slap them both. I felt as though pieces of me were free-floating in space, and every time I reached out to grab one and attach it to the rest of me, it slipped away.

If I wasn't an incest survivor, if I wasn't Jane's lover, who was I?

If I didn't live on Planet Incest anymore, if I wasn't a citizen of Lesbian Nation anymore, where did I belong?

If my recovered memories weren't true, why had I wrecked my family?

Matthew and Charlie were surprisingly unsurprised by Jane's disappearance. I told them Jane and I had broken up, and they didn't ask why. Charlie asked when he'd see her. I told him I didn't know. I didn't tell him that I also didn't know where she was living or whether I'd ever hear from her again. I gave him her phone number at work and told him he could call her if he wanted to.

"I want her to call me," he said.

"I know," I said. "I'm sorry." *I'm so sorry, Charlie.*

I stashed the fourth kitchen chair in the attic. Without question or comment, Matthew set the table each night for three.

Jane and I had been so careful not to fight when the kids were with us. Had they overheard more of our craziness than I'd let myself admit? Were they relieved that it was finally over? Glad to have their mother's undivided attention again?

Charlie and Matthew were nearly men now, sixteen and seventeen, both six-feet-one-inch tall. Maybe now that they were within spitting distance of their own adult lives, they were less interested in the vicissitudes of mine.

Maybe biology truly was destiny, and no amount of lesbian-family picnics in Cedar-Rose Park and alternative-family bedtime stories could make losing their "other mother" of twelve years matter as much to them as losing the nuclear family that had included their dad.

Or maybe being three—Mom in the middle, one tall man-child on each side—felt stable, safe, and sane to them, as it did, unexpectedly, to me.

It took a few months, a few pharmaceutical interventions, and a few dozen sessions with Miranda, but finally I began to feel like a person with a future.

A future, and an unresolved past. Jane was gone, and so was my belief that my father had molested me. It was time to talk to my dad.

I considered showing up on his doorstep. But after my bailout on the phone a year ago, I was afraid he'd turn me away. I considered calling him, but I was afraid he'd hang up on me again.

E-mail would measure out a safer distance, but I barely knew how to use it myself. As a seventy-year-old who embodied the Jewish male stereotype, my father was probably still composing his endless to-do lists on a Smith-Corona.

So I headed back to Walgreens' card aisle, where I saw that my window of opportunity was still open: there was still no line of Hallmark incest cards. I bought a "Thinking of You on Your Birthday" card, blank inside.

"Dad," I wrote, "I'm sorry about what happened the last time you called. If you're willing to try again, please call me when you can."

I signed it "Love, Meredith." And I meant it.

The New York Times
July 2, 1996
"In Research Scans, Telltale Signs Sort False Memories from True"

For the first time, scientists may have captured snapshots of a false memory in the making.

In computer-enhanced images produced by a technique known as PET scanning, for positron emission tomography, researchers have made pictures of the brain at work recalling a memory, and pictures of the brain going awry and bringing up a false memory. . . . In the images produced by these new brain scans, false memories can be clearly distinguished from those that are true.

. . . The field of memory research was rocked by several criminal prosecutions in the 1980s and early 1990s that were based partly on "recovered memories." A survey in 1994 by the National Center on Child Abuse and Neglect suggested that more than 12,000 similar accusations—including ritual satanic abuse based on such "recovered memories"—had been brought nationwide, even though, the survey said, none had been substantiated by physical evidence.

—Philip J. Hilts

Progress. This time when I heard my father's voice on the phone I could talk to him standing up.

"I was glad to get your card, Meredith," he said. This time his voice was guarded, careful, not angry. "I was wondering . . . would you like to come over for a swim on Sunday? You're welcome to bring Jane and the boys."

I took a deep breath. "Jane and I broke up."

"I'm sorry to hear that," he said.

No you're not, I thought.

I'd spent nearly a decade wearing incest-colored glasses, reevaluating everything my father had ever said and done through a filter of suspicion and blame. If I wanted to reconcile with him, undo the damage I'd done, I needed to turn that scrutiny on myself instead.

"We'll see you Sunday," I said.

My dad.

There he was, weaving his way through the poolside chaises: navy blue swim trunks, bare feet, unsteady smile.

He was grayer than I'd remembered him. Balder. Shorter. He'd been so much bigger in my head.

"Hello, Meredith."

"Hello, Dad." We reached for each other, squirmed in and quickly out of an awkward hug.

Of course he's afraid to touch me, I thought. The impact of the fracture I'd caused, the knitting together that had yet to happen and might never happen, hit me in a way it hadn't before. I felt a wave of nausea: mourning sickness.

"Hi, Grandpa," Matthew said into the silence. He wrapped his furry blonde arms around my father's furry gray chest. My father patted him on the back and turned to Charlie.

Charlie stuck his hand out. He and my father shook hands, like men.

Silence again.

"Did you bring your suits?" my father asked. Eager to escape the tension, Matthew and Charlie tossed their T-shirts and flip-flops onto the nearest chaise and chased each other into the pool. Matthew dove in. Charlie cannonballed, a loud, wet, smacking splat. "Beat you to the other side," Charlie shouted, and the two of them raced the length of the pool, all whitewater and bobbing heads and big flashing feet.

I turned to my father, wanting him to say how wonderful they were. I wanted him to be as moved as I was by the smooth locomotion of their strong young muscles, the beauty of their blooming bodies.

"I saved us a spot," my father said instead. He led me across the hot cement to two chaises pushed close together, one partially shaded by the umbrella overhead. He arranged his fleshy body on the shaded chaise. He didn't have to ask which one I wanted. He knew I loved to lie in the sun.

Eight years apart, ten minutes together, and already I could taste the ambrosia and the poison of our relationship: He knows me; he knows me too well.

The two of us lay there, side by side on sticky vinyl chaises, our bodies dripping sweat, our faces turned away from each other, his eyes shaded by the umbrella, my eyes closed against the sun.

"The boys are so tall," my father said.

"They have a competition going," I said. "Mom's got a chart on her kitchen wall."

"Who's winning?" my father asked. A small grin played at the corners of his mouth. You've got your father's mouth, people used to tell me. Charlie had that mouth, too.

"What are you doing, handicapping my kids?" I teased him back.

"Depends. Who's the favorite?" he said.

I was always your favorite, I thought. *And we all paid the price.*

"It's neck and neck," I said.

My father gestured at the kids in the pool. Matthew's sun-streaked hair streamed halfway down his back. Drops of water stuck to the stubble of Charlie's shaved head.

"Hair and head, you mean," my father said, and I turned toward him and rolled my eyes, and we laughed together.

We spent the afternoon and the next several years that way: making jokes, making new memories, making our way back to each other—no questions answered, no questions asked.

eleven

~~What~~ Was I Thinking?

Aligning ourselves with our injuries only benefits us
for so long. Ultimately, a label that initially brought
strength, solidarity and understanding can become
a prison from which we must free ourselves.
—*Laura Davis (coauthor of* The Courage to Heal),
I Thought We'd Never Speak Again:
The Road from Estrangement
to Reconciliation, 2002

In some families, letting sleeping dogs lie (and lying daughters
off the hook) would be normal behavior: discretion the better
part of valor, a civil buttoning up of the stiff upper lip. But in
my big-mouthed, New York Jewish family of origin, silence has
always been a hole to fill, discretion the purview of cultures alien
to ours.

So it was utterly out of character that in the years since my
father and I had reconciled, not one relative of mine had wondered—aloud, at least—what the hell I'd been thinking when I'd
accused my father of molesting me, if indeed I'd been thinking
at all, and what the hell I was thinking about it now.

Post-estrangement, we'd resumed family business as usual. In
various configurations of parents and grandparents and cousins
and aunts and uncle, we'd gone back to betting on the horses at
Bay Meadows, taking shorter and shorter walks at my father's

slowing pace, gorging ourselves at the groaning board of my father's favorite all-you-can-eat Sunday brunch. As he always had, my father handicapped the races and brought the bagels and cracked the jokes. Father and daughter, brother and sister, siblings and cousins laughed and argued and worried and bored each other, the way normal families do.

In the intervening years I'd raised two teenagers, which is to say I'd matriculated at the college of parental hard knocks, with a double major in midnight floor-pacing and humility. Charlie's adolescence had not been an easy one, and many of the professionals involved—school administrators, therapists, and then officers of the juvenile court—had taken to blaming his behavior on me.

"It's because your mom's a lesbian, isn't it?" Charlie's county-appointed probation officer asked him when I was out of the room.

"You were too lenient. Too strict. Too laid back. Too over-protective," one expert after another informed me. Charlie was acting out because I'd deprived him of male role models. Abandoned him by taking a full-time job. Sacrificed his economic stability to pursue my freelance career.

Charlie's troubles flipped my script on parental culpability. I loved my sons with animal ferocity, and despite the sucking vortex of maternal guilt, I knew I was a good mother. Not the best mother in human history, surely; surely not the worst. But if I didn't want to be fully responsible for Charlie's troubles, how could I hold my father fully responsible for mine?

I didn't know whether to credit grace or encroaching senility, but as Charlie's adolescent storm raged on, my dad had never uttered the obvious: *now you know what you put me through.* He didn't have to. I got it, and I tried again and again to tell my father so.

But my dad, that handicapper of thoroughbreds, didn't want to "beat a dead horse," as he'd said. He'd changed the subject every time I'd brought it up.

"I owe you an apology, Dad," I said one Sunday while he and Gloria and I were plowing through overflowing plates of "salad" at his new favorite eatery, Fresh Choice.

My father's fork, loaded with potato salad smothered in bacon bits, paused en route to his mouth. "So *you're* the one who stole the cheese toast off my plate."

He turned to Gloria, his face contorted in mock remorse. "I owe *you* an apology. I blamed you."

"Forgiven." Gloria scooped up her "diet salad," syrupy peach slices clinging to curds of cottage cheese.

"I'm serious, Dad," I persisted. "I accused you of doing something terrible to me. And I was wrong."

My father put his fork down, wiped his mouth, and pushed back his chair. "If they're out of cheese toast, someone's in trouble," he said, and went back to the salad bar.

After Jane, I took the bitter vow of the heartbroken and swore I'd never fall in love again. The rubble was still smoldering one year later when a friend offered to set me up with a lesbian who was visiting the Bay Area from France.

"She's perfect for you," my friend said. "Katrine is beautiful. Smart. Funny. She lives in Paris, but she comes to Berkeley a couple of times a year."

Funny, schmunny. Katrine *did* sound perfect—because she lived a continent and an ocean away.

A meeting was arranged. Putting my worst foot forward, offering a kind of preemptive warning, I arrived very late. And took one look at the very annoyed Frenchwoman in question. And felt that arrow's familiar sting.

By the time Katrine flew back to Paris three weeks later, I'd broken my vow and made a new one: to take a chance on her, on myself. Katrine and I were too good together to pass up. It would be different this time, I told myself. *I* would be different this time. Anyway, a repeat performance of my last relationship wasn't possible with Katrine. She was the anti-Jane.

Katrine had grown up in Normandy, playing in the minefields the Germans had left behind. The front door of her family home was still pocked by the Nazi bullets that had killed her great-grandparents, executed for hiding Resistance fighters during the war.

Katrine knew the difference between real and imagined suffering. She lacked the victimhood gene. She remembered exactly what had happened in her childhood and she knew that it sucked, as many childhoods do. She smelled exotically European, sexy sweat with an overlay of Hermès perfume. She laughed heartily and easily and often. And she'd never been in a therapist's office in her life.

Seven months and eight hundred pages of love-faxes later, Katrine had left France to come and make a life with me. Matthew had moved to Hawaii the day after his high school graduation, making his surfer-boy dream come true. Seventeen-year-old Charlie, his teenage inferno in full flame, was living with me between stints in Juvenile Hall.

Katrine couldn't wait to meet my father. Nervously, I arranged a lunch. Within minutes the two of them were talking and laughing, old friends on first encounter. She and Gloria joked in French about my father and me, rolling their eyes at the crazy Americans they loved.

"Your dad's so clever and funny," Katrine told me on the way home. "Just like you. Now I see where you get your wacky sense of humor. And your beautiful lips and shiny brown eyes."

"Aww," I demurred, "you say that to all the American girls."

"Only this American girl," Katrine assured me.

Later that night, my father called. "Katrine's so great," he said.

I nearly dropped the phone. Was my father really accepting—*approving of*—a lover of mine? What's next, I wondered, world peace?

"She's a wonderful addition to the family," he announced: case closed, competition over.

Seven years later, on a brilliant blue-sky day in February 2003, in the great room of a friend's home overlooking Tomales Bay, Katrine and I got as married as two women could.

At twenty-three, Charlie had outgrown his adolescence; he was a Christian minister now, a counselor of teenagers in an inner-city drug rehab facility. Standing at a rented podium in a three-piece suit, he performed the wedding ceremony. Matthew read a poem he'd written, rhyming "So glad they met" with "Katrine's famous vinaigrette."

My whole family watched, beaming and weeping, as the strains of Mendelssohn's Wedding March filled the room. My seventy-six-year-old dad, stooped, shuffling, and somber, walked me down the aisle.

Juvenile Justice Bulletin
(U.S. Department of Justice)
January 2004
"Explanations for the Decline in Child Sexual Abuse Cases"

The number of sexual abuse cases substantiated by child protective service agencies (CPS) dropped a remarkable 40 percent between 1992 and 2000, from an estimated 150,000 cases to 89,500 cases, but professional opinion is divided about why. It is possible that the incidence of sexual abuse has declined as a result of two decades of prevention, treatment, and aggressive criminal justice activity. It is also possible that there has been no real decline, and that the apparent decline is explained by a drop in the number of cases being identified and reported....

> The possibility that a real decline occurred is heartening and could point the way to more effective strategies for preventing all kinds of child maltreatment. On the other hand, if the decline is due solely to decreased reporting . . . it could mean that more children are failing to get the help and services they need.
>
> —David Finkelhor and Lisa M. Jones

My father and Gloria and I were having brunch at an upscale hotel buffet on a Sunday morning in 2005, cracking crab legs the size of swing-arm lamps, bloodying our plates with thick hunks of prime rib.

My father was telling Gloria about a magazine he'd worked for as a young man, the name of which had slipped his mind. He turned to me. "You remember, Shirley," he said. "I got that job when you were pregnant with Meredith."

For years Gloria had been telling my brother and me that our dad was becoming dangerously absentminded, that he didn't always know where he was. You don't know him the way we do, my brother and I kept arguing. He's always had the attention span of a hummingbird with ADHD. This is nothing new, we said.

I put my crab pick down. This was something new.

"Dad," I said. "I'm your daughter. Not your ex-wife."

My father blinked. "When your mother was pregnant with you, I mean," he said.

Who doesn't mix things up at age seventy-eight? I soothed myself. I clung to that thought for as long as I could. And then a couple of weeks later, when my father and I were talking on the phone, he asked if I wanted to do something with him, and he couldn't think of the word for what it was.

"Dinner?" I asked. It had to involve food. "Dim sum?"

Suddenly: Bad Dad. "You know what I'm talking about," he snapped.

"If I knew, I'd tell you," I said.

I heard pain in my father's silence. *Sad Dad.* "The place with the horses," he said, his voice quavering.

"The *racetrack?*"

"Of course," my father said impatiently.

And then one day a few months later, my phone rang, and my caller ID said, S MARAN, and it wasn't my dad but Gloria calling.

"We just came from the gerontologist," Gloria said. "It's Alzheimer's, Mer."

My brain did a mad dash to denial. "Shouldn't we get a second opinion?"

"Meredith." Gloria's voice was firm. "There's no question that your father has this disease. He might go on as he is for some time. Or he might get worse very quickly."

We've wasted so much time, I thought. *I've* wasted so much time.

This wasn't like the other times I'd lost my father—when I'd moved away from him, when he'd moved away from me. This time, he wouldn't be coming back.

The Los Angeles Times Magazine
October 30, 2005
"I'm Sorry: An Introduction"

Twenty-one years ago, a child then known as Kyle Sapp told police that he had been the victim of sexual abuse at the McMartin Pre-School in Manhattan Beach. Sapp, who attended the preschool from 1979 to 1980, was 8 when he first talked to authorities in 1984.

... In the decade and a half since the defendants were set free, research psychologists have shown that it's easy to pressure children to describe bad things that never happened. False memories can feel real, though, not just for preschoolers but for older children as well. But Sapp, now known as Kyle Zirpolo, says he never had false memories: He always knew his stories of abuse were made up.

"I've got two little kids I love dearly—they've changed the priorities in my life," Zirpolo says. "My goal is to raise them as best as I can and try to lead by example. I want to be totally honest with them, to say, 'This is something that happened to me. I did something dishonest, then at some point I was able to be honest about it.'"

The adults at the McMartin Pre-School "never did anything to me, and I never saw them doing anything," he says today. "I said a lot of things that didn't happen. I lied."

—Debbie Nathan

Two of the McMartins had died before they could hear Zirpolo's apology. I didn't want my father to die—or lose his mind to Alzheimer's—before he could hear mine.

The New York Times
February 3, 2007
"A Study of Memory Looks at Fact and Fiction"

In . . . the current issue of *Psychological Medicine*, a team of psychiatrists and literary scholars reports that it could not find a single account of repressed memory, fictional or not, before the year 1800.

The researchers offered a $1,000 reward last March to anyone who could document such a case in a healthy, lucid person. None of the responses were convincing, the authors wrote, suggesting that repressed memory is a "culture-bound syndrome" and not a natural process of human memory.

—Benedict Carey

> **The New York Times**
> April 5, 2008
> **"52 Girls Are Taken from Mormon
> Sect's Ranch in Texas"**
>
> Responding to an accusation of sexual abuse of a 16-year-old girl, Texas enforcement officers and child welfare investigators raided a West Texas ranch founded by the convicted polygamist sect leader Warren Jeffs and removed 52 children, officials said Friday.
>
> ...The raid, which began late Thursday, stemmed from a complaint to child and family services on Monday that a 16-year-old girl at the ranch had been sexually and physically abused.
>
> —*Ralph Blumenthal*

From: "Larry"@aol.com

Date: December 31, 2008 1:01:17 A.M. PST

To: Meredith@MeredithMaran.com

Subject: SOS

Hi Meredith,

It's 1:00am on New Year's Eve, and I just read your Brides Magazine article "When a Sexually Abused Child Weds" and . . . just about every line in the article described my relationship with my wife to the T. You see, until a year ago, my wife had no idea of what had happened to her as a child. Actually, sexually abused is a real "kind" word to describe what happened to my sweet wife. She was a sex slave to a whole Mormon community for 13 years of her life.

We have 3 beautiful, amazing, daughters, and we have always had the most real, spectacular love and understanding for each other and our children. We built a great life together, and then in the blink of an eye, everything got turned upside down, as she started remembering. And now on Jan 1st, 1 year later, my sweetheart is in the hospital, because she was spinning out of control and putting herself in dangerous situations.

. . . I am sending out an SOS. I don't know where you are or how to get in touch with you but I can be reached at the info below. . . .

"Larry"

Twenty-four years after publishing my first incest exposé, I was still getting e-mails from people like Larry who'd read the articles online and wanted my help.

I wasn't an incest therapist; I just played one on the Internet. But reading the letters was wrenching. I wished I could do *something* to help.

Twenty-four years later I was still a journalist, still deciphering the world and my place in it as a journalist does: fingers on keyboard, ear to the ground. I decided to look for answers to Larry's questions and my own in that way. Where to start?

Praise be to Google: I found my long-ago co-counselor, Catherine, still living in California, still working as a radio producer, making programs about the environment now, not child sexual abuse. She drove to Oakland from her home in the mountains and we settled onto my couch, the way we used to do in the good-bad old days.

I opened a bottle of Trader Joe's finest $3 Chardonnay and raised a toast. "To surviving," I said, irony intended. We clinked glasses, smiled, drank, made small talk, and then Catherine asked me, "Do you still think your dad molested you?"

"Nope." I refilled our glasses. "You?"

"Nope," Catherine answered.

We stared at each other for a long moment.

"Of all the women I know who accused their fathers back then," Catherine said, "only one of them still believes it's true."

"I don't know a single person who still believes her accusation," I said.

"What about Jane?" Catherine asked.

"We hardly talk." I was stabbed by curiosity. Could Jane still believe that she'd been abused by a murderous satanic cult?

"A couple of years after I accused my dad," Catherine said, "my parents split up. My mother still blames me. She says I drove a wedge between her and my father."

Catherine and I started swapping "retractor" stories. My friend Heidi had realized her accusation was false before she'd made it public. Catherine's friend Georgia had divorced her husband because he didn't believe her accusation, then realized, too late, that her husband was right. Jackie's father had died before he could meet his grandchildren, or hear his daughter's apology.

Nicole believed that her breast cancer diagnosis was "payback" for the allegations she'd made against her father in 1989. "I poisoned my family," she'd told me. "And I poisoned my own heart." Diane's incest accusation had prompted her father's suicide. At his funeral, she'd realized it wasn't true.

Catherine pulled a battered journal out of her backpack. "I'll show you mine if you show me yours," she said.

I opened my own journal, newly retrieved from the trunk where I'd kept it for the past twenty years. The two of us flipped through our journals, one page at a time, comparing and contrasting. Catherine's incest dreams mirrored mine. Catherine's lists of "evidence" looked just like mine. Her handwriting was tight and tidy at the tops of the pages, looping off the bottom in a childish scrawl, just like mine.

"Freaky," Catherine said.

"Do you think we were brainwashed?" I wondered aloud. "Or did we brainwash ourselves?"

Catherine frowned. "I don't see what we did as an entirely bad thing. There were excesses for sure—"

"You think?"

"But we saved lives, too. We made the culture rethink the way families relate to each other. People believe kids, now, when they say they're being abused."

Catherine swirled pale wine in her glass. "I got a lot out of it. It was a mess, and a mistake. But getting through it taught me to believe myself. I found my voice and I used it. That matters more to me than whether or not what I was saying was true."

I was half-impressed, half-appalled by Catherine's take-no-prisoners honesty. But wait. She *had* taken prisoners. "What about all the people who got hurt?"

"My parents had a terrible marriage long before I accused my dad. The truth is, they're better off apart."

"Whose truth is that?" I asked. "Yours? Or theirs?"

Catherine set her glass down on the coffee table. "When I worked with Judy Chicago in the late seventies," she said, "she told me that no matter how close you get to the truth, you'll be called a liar because yours is always different from someone else's. What matters is that you tell your own authentic story. And that's what we did."

Honesty. Authenticity. Story. Lie. Truth. The words swam in my head, arranging and rearranging themselves like the poetry word-magnets on my fridge.

"But we *lied*," I said.

"I didn't lie," Catherine said. "I said what I believed to be true at the time."

She peered at me. "So did you," she said. "You were *tortured* about your estrangement from your dad. You wouldn't have gone through all that if you hadn't believed your father molested you. You can't tell me otherwise. I was there, remember?"

I saw myself in the ex-house I'd shared with my ex-lover on my ex-couch with Catherine, my ex-counselor: telling her my incest dreams, shaking with my incest fears, sobbing out my incest grief.

True then, false now?

Literally true then, emotionally true now?

False then, false now?

"I remember," I said.

My ex-therapist, Ruth, had been there, too, plumbing the depths of my incest-obsessed head. So I broke my no-therapy rule and called her old number, which was still her number, and made an appointment to see her.

Ruth's wood-paneled waiting room was the same, the neatly fanned display of *The New Yorkers* and *The Atlantic* on the coffee table was the same, and even Ruth was the same: more salt than pepper in her hair, now, but still the shawl of flowing fabric, still the blue-eyed welcoming smile.

"It's been a long time," she said, folding her hands, waiting, with that I've-got-all-day-for-you look on her face—the look that used to soothe me instantly. It soothed me still.

I filled her in on my project. "Can you help me remember myself back then?" I asked.

"I don't remember the details of our work together," Ruth said slowly. A small smile played at her lips. "But right now I'm aware of wanting to pull up a memory and tell you what you want to hear—whether it's true or not."

She laughed. I laughed. All those years later, we were on the same side again.

"I do remember you talking to me about *The Courage to Heal*. I remember feeling incredibly conflicted," she said. "I was trained as a Jungian, with an emphasis on following the client's psyche, not imposing an idea of mine about where the client should go.

"On the other hand, it seemed very true to me that a lot of children are sexually abused, and you might have been one of them. If that was true, I would have been failing you by hanging out with the not knowing.

"There was so much pressure during those years to try and find incest memories in every client," she continued. "In the therapeutic community in the late 1980s and early 1990s, incest was this cookie-cutter answer to every woman's problems. If I questioned that, at a conference or even in a private conversation, I'd be accused of being a bad therapist. It was very polarizing.

"There was an atmosphere of certainty about things I couldn't agree with. People in the field were saying that children never lie, that if a woman had incest dreams, it meant she'd been molested."

"I believed that," I said. "As you might recall."

"It was hard to believe anything else in those days," Ruth said. "But children do lie. And dreams with an incest theme are common among women who are longing to be more connected to their fathers, or who are too connected to their fathers, or whose fathers are too connected to them."

Longing to be more connected to my father. Check.

Being too connected to my father; my father being too connected to me. *More like entangled than connected*, I thought. But yes. Check.

"There are fads and fashions in the therapeutic community," Ruth said. "Now it's all about brain research. People aren't so interested in slogging through the unconscious and connecting it with consciousness." She grinned ruefully. "Which happens to be what I do for a living."

I asked if clients still came to her chasing incest memories.

"I'm not seeing as many incest survivors as I saw in the eighties," Ruth answered. "But when I do, it doesn't feel like they're going on a fishing expedition just because it's de rigueur.

"Twenty years ago you believed your clients' memories, or said you did, no matter how far-fetched they seemed. Since then, a lot of my clients have realized that their memories were metaphorically true, or emotionally true, but not literally true.

"I want to validate and support my clients, but I won't be a party to false allegations anymore. In the therapeutic community, no one wants to talk about our role in the sex-panic that started twenty years ago. So we haven't been able to help each other figure out how to walk that tightrope now."

"When did you start thinking of it as a sex-panic?"

Ruth ran manicured fingers through the silky folds of her shawl. "The turning point was a *New Yorker* story that came out in '92 or '93, about an incest case that turned out to be about false memories."

"'Remembering Satan,' by Lawrence Wright," I said.

"Right." Ruth nodded. "All the therapists were talking about it. I felt this enormous sweeping relief. I could finally let go of the burden I'd been carrying: that I wasn't being there for my patients because I didn't want to push an idea into their psyches."

I asked if she thought the term *mass hysteria* was an apt description of that time. "Absolutely," she answered. "A lot of people and families were hurt. Enormous damage was done to innocent sensual connection between adults and children.

"At the same time, there was a lot of sexual abuse of children that was coming into consciousness. It was very important that it did."

Ruth leaned forward in her chair. "I just *recovered a memory* of our work together. I remember thinking that whether or not you'd been molested, what you really wanted was for your father to *see* you—not for his own gratification, but for the person you were."

"He sees me now." I considered this. "As much as he can," I added.

"I'm so happy to hear that." I caught Ruth glancing at her watch in that not-so-subtle way of hers. She caught me catching her, and smiled, that warm smile.

"It's been lovely to see you again," she said. Translation: my time was up.

I scrambled to turn off my tape recorder and cram my laptop into its bag, berating myself for breaking the therapy client's cardinal rule: never be caught mid-emotion at the fifty-minute mark.

Ruth stood. "This is such an important topic," she said. "I'm so glad you're writing about it."

As I stood up I noticed that there *was* something new in Ruth's office: a little red light blinking above the doorway. Her next client was waiting, hoping to drop a few ounces of whatever weight she was carrying during her fifty minutes in this room.

"It's been great to see you too," I said.

Time Magazine
April 28, 2008
"Cellar Incest Case Shocks Austria"

For almost a quarter of a century . . . Elisabeth Fritzl was enduring an unimaginable ordeal behind the plain gray walls of a nondescript house.

Her 73-year-old father, Josef, today confessed that he held his now 42-year-old daughter captive for 24 years in a concealed, windowless basement hideout, where he repeatedly had sexual intercourse with her and where she gave birth to seven of his children.

Elizabeth Fritzl . . . was 11 years old when her father raped her for the first time. Josef Fritzl appears to have meticulously carried out his deed while acting like a caring father. His wife, who insists that she had no idea what was going on in the house, was never allowed to set foot in the basement. . . .

—*Stephanie Kirchner*

Catherine and Ruth had seen me through my crazy time, but there was only one person who'd lived it with me. Twelve years after our breakup, Jane and I owned houses a mile apart. We still shared custody of the no-hot-water, no-electricity country cabin we'd bought together in 1988, because neither of us could bear to give up her half-share.

Jane still saw Charlie regularly, Matthew rarely. She and I had tried to be friends (too much history, too little in common), coparents to Matthew and Charlie (overly ambitious and, now that the boys were nearly men, age-inappropriate), or, at least, *civil* when we were brought together by kid- or cabin-related events.

So it was with no small amount of trepidation that I called Jane and asked if we could get together. If she was curious about my agenda, she didn't say so. She asked only when and where.

I found her sitting at a small round table at a brewpub in downtown Berkeley, stirring milk into a mug of—if memory and olfactory sensors served—English breakfast tea. She looked exactly the same as she had the last time I'd seen her, years ago. I wondered if I looked the same to her.

We exchanged an awkward half-hug and then we sat down and she asked me why I'd called.

"After we broke up," I began, "I realized that my father never molested me." I checked her face for storm clouds brewing. Nothing. Yet.

"I'm trying to understand why I accused him," I went on. "I'm hoping you can help. Anything you can remember . . ."

Jane picked at her napkin. "The way my mind works," she said, "it's best if I just tell you everything I remember, in no particular order."

I nodded, grateful for her willingness to help, pen poised over pad.

"When we first met, you were editing Roselyn Taylor's incest book," she said. "I remember us saying how strange it was that of all the streets in Oakland, she happened to live on Taylor Street."

Roselyn lived on McKinley Street. She still does.

"You talked about how your father always hated all your boyfriends and disrespected your husband to his face. You told me he took you to the Kentucky Derby, just the two of you, when you were ten. He got drunk. You were afraid."

I'd called this meeting hoping that Jane would help me recover true memories of my false memories. But now that we were here together, what I was remembering was the agony and the ecstasy of being her lover. The way she'd held me, and my pain, so close. The way she'd analyzed me so authoritatively, making me feel more loved than I'd ever felt, and as invaded as my father had always made me feel.

"You were his precious, difficult, favorite child," Jane was saying. "He was withholding, hard to please. He'd grace you with material things if you performed well for him. You didn't like the power dynamic. You hated the control he had over you.

"The first time I met your father, he sat me down for the typical son-in-law interview. He asked me where I worked and what I did. When I told him, he asked me why I wasn't president of the company yet. 'Don't you have any aspirations?' he asked me, five minutes after we first laid eyes on each other.

"His possessiveness was your biggest clue when you started thinking he'd molested you: 'Nobody's good enough for you. You're *mine.*'"

Jane stroked her teacup with those long, slender fingers of hers. "You never said you were sure," she continued. "But it was clear that you were absolutely traumatized."

It was?

"Did you believe that my father had molested me?" I asked.

"I knew that men like your father molest their daughters," Jane answered without hesitation. "I also knew that you were surrounded by people working on incest, and headlines about incest. There was a very painful place in you that you were trying to figure out. A bunch of circumstances pointed you in that direction.

"I could believe that he'd abused you. I could also believe that you were just stitching things together, your own life and your journalism, the way you always do."

I took a step into dangerous territory. "What do you think about *your* accusations?" I asked. "What do you think happened to you?"

Jane stared into her teacup. Who could blame her for not wanting to answer the question that had broken us up? "Why do you want to know?" she asked.

"Your story is part of my story," I said.

I watched her turning this over in her mind. "I know now that my abuse wasn't satanic," she said. "But I know for a fact that my memories are true."

Now it was my turn to avert my eyes. What had I expected? Not this.

"How do you know that?" I asked, and Jane told me about a trip she'd made to her hometown after we broke up. She'd spent hours reading microfiche in her hometown library, she said. She'd found a fire circle in the woods near her childhood home.

How can she not remember that we were still together when she took that trip? Did she think it was her new girlfriend who'd been waiting for her call each night? Her new girlfriend hearing the story she was telling me for the second time?

My incest memories had always been vague; my dad's intentions open to interpretation. Emotional incest: debatable. Sadomasochistic ritual abuse: not so much. Either Jane's father and his fellow cult members had raped her, or they hadn't.

"Are you still . . . working on your healing?" I asked her instead.

Jane shook her head. "It's as if I climbed a mountain I had to climb. Now I'm on the other side. Life is easier here."

"I'm glad for you," I said—the truth.

No wonder we'd all gone nuts on Planet Incest, trying to distinguish memories from imaginings, truth from lies. Incest is the perfect false accusation for the victimhood seeker, just as it's the perpetrator's perfect crime. Beatings leave bruises. Neglect sends kids to school with tattered clothes. But I couldn't have proved that my father had molested me, just as he couldn't have proved that he hadn't.

When my father kissed me—on the forehead, on the cheek, on the lips—was he expressing love, or lust? When my father inserted himself into my every thought, feeling, decision, was he being attentive, or emotionally abusing me?

I paid the check, and Jane walked me to my car. "Charlie told me that your father's not doing so well," she said as I was fumbling with my keys. "I'm sorry to hear that."

She put her hands on my shoulders, the way she used to when my shoulders were hers to touch, and gazed intently into my eyes.

"Take good care of yourself, Meredith," she said.

"I will," I said, leaning in toward her—old habit. Then I slipped into the driver's seat and drove away, feeling guilty—survivor's guilt—and relieved.

twelve

Eternal Sunshine of the Recovered Mind

Amnesia for childhood sexual abuse is a condition.
The existence of this condition is beyond dispute.
. . . At least 10% of people sexually abused in
childhood will have periods of complete
amnesia for their abuse, followed by experiences
of delayed recall.

—*Jim Hopper, Ph.D., Harvard Medical School,*
"Recovered Memories of Sexual Abuse;
Scientific Research and Scholarly Resources,"
http://www.jimhopper.com, September 27, 2008

In this book, I will describe the calamitous course
of the recovered memory movement in psychiatric
practice and how the theories on which it was
based proved invalid and pernicious.
—*Paul McHugh, M.D., Johns Hopkins Medical School,*
Try to Remember, *November 2008*

I'd had too much therapy to look to the couch for answers. Yes,
my accusation was the product of a custom-constructed constel-
lation of neuroses and family dynamics unique to me and mine.
But there had been too many preschool kids like Kyle Zirpolo,
too many adults like me telling the same lie at the same time to
blame the particulars of my situation.

There was a bigger picture, and I wanted to see it, and I wanted someone I trusted to show it to me.

I'd been reading and admiring Katha Pollitt for years. Described by *The New York Review of Books* as "A good old-fashioned feminist and leftist columnist for *The Nation*, as well as a prize-winning poet," Pollitt had also been a loud voice in the memory war, writing often about falsely accused "abusers" who remained imprisoned. She'd focused on Bernard Baran, an openly gay child-care worker who'd served twenty-two years since his arrest at age nineteen.

I e-mailed Pollitt, asking for her thoughts about feminists' role in sending innocent people to jail. "I'm troubled that you single out the feminist movement," Pollitt responded. "The police, prosecutors and judges in these cases were mostly men, often very conservative men, local district attorneys and politicians making their careers with a high-profile case.

"The media that ran with sensational stories is run by men who are hardly feminist. The feminist insights that molestation and incest are more common than once believed were used in the day-care cases to serve a conservative agenda: day-care is bad (mom should be home), the world is dangerous (you need more law and order), and even nice-seeming people are really predators (so don't let your kids out of your sight)."

I asked what and whom Pollitt blamed for the sex-panic. "Blaming 'the enemy within' is pretty familiar," she answered. "In America we have a long Puritan history that has shaped the way we think about sex. In the case of day-care panic, add Puritanism to the anxiety and guilt of working mothers, and fears about putting kids into care, and the general feeling that day care is low-quality, second-best to family care.

"And of course sexual abuse of children and women is very common. So that's something people carry around with them.

"That said," Pollitt continued, "the feminist movement brought to light the tremendous amount of abuse of children and women in our society. Previously victims had often been dismissed as crazy or lying or at fault.

"Out of that sense of solidarity with victims came the idea that those who claimed victimization were always telling the literal truth—believe the woman, believe the children.

"What got left out is that some of the accusations were constructed—by 'recovered memory' therapists and therapists who just assumed all kinds of problems were proof of molestation, and by the police and prosecutors in the case of the day-care panic cases."

"Any thoughts about preventing another episode like this?" I wrote her.

"I think implementing better police techniques is crucial to preventing another outbreak," she answered. "Videotaping interviews, for example. If the jury had seen what the therapist in the Baran case did to get the kids to say what she wanted them to, they might have been more skeptical.

"But if you look at who gets convicted, it's mostly not people with a lot of social standing, sophistication or money for lawyers. Bernard Baran was a gay working class teenager; his mother sold her car for $500 to pay legal fees. This kind of person is easy pickings for prosecution."

National Center for Reason and Justice
June 30, 2006
"Bernard Baran Released After Nearly 22 Years in Prison: New Trial Ordered by Massachusetts Superior Court Judge"

Boston—A Massachusetts judge has ordered a new trial for Bernard Baran, who has been in prison for almost 22 years.

Baran's 1985 conviction on mass molestation charges was overturned last week when a new trial was ordered by Superior Court Judge Francis R. Fecteau.

The judge ruled that Baran's original attorney provided incompetent counsel, raising questions about whether Baran got a fair trial.

I wasn't the only feminist who'd reevaluated her stance. In the latest, 1999 edition of Diana Russell's book *The Secret Trauma: Incest in the Lives of Girls and Women*, first published at the height of the panic in 1986, I found a surprising new introduction.

The Secret Trauma, Revised Edition
1999
"The Great Incest Wars: Against Polarization"

In the years following the publication of *The Secret Trauma*, the debate over incest escalated into a momentous and venomous controversy.

"The memory wars," or "the Great Incest War," as these battles have been called, pitted the child sexual abuse incest recovery movement against the false memory movement.

While . . . incest is a widespread and urgent problem, I now believe that both sides of "the Great Incest War" have some validity as well as many shortcomings. I also believe that both sides have undermined the feminist effort that first brought incest to public attention.

I believe that therapists in the incest recovery movement were the first culprits responsible for subverting the feminist incest revolution and transforming it into a counter revolution.

My thinking changed radically when I read lengthy personal accounts by retractors who had retrieved "memories" of incestuous abuse and/or satanic ritual abuse in therapy only to denounce them as false later in their lives.

—*Diana E. H. Russell*

Diana Russell—against polarization? I could more easily imagine the pope opposing prayer.

Amazon.com
November 15, 2008
"Product Description of *Try to Remember:*
Psychiatry's Clash over Meaning, Memory,
and *Mind*, by Paul McHugh"

An urgent call to arms for patients and therapists alike, *Try to Remember* delineates the difference between good and bad psychiatry and challenges us to reconsider psychotherapy as the most effective way to heal troubled minds.

"Of all the mad ideas that have swept through the practice of psychiatry since Freud . . . none has resulted in more cruelty to patients and their loved ones than those that led to the Recovered Memory Movement."—Midge Dector

"This is the absorbing, never-before-told story of how a cult of Freudian psychiatrists went on a witch-hunt across America, before a small band of scientists risked their reputations and livelihoods to expose the cult for what it was: a wacky pack a quacks."—Tom Wolfe

I e-mailed Jennifer Freyd to ask if I could interview her about her accusation against her father, FMSF cofounder Peter Freyd. She told me that she no longer discusses her family of origin in public.

Her estranged mother, Pamela Freyd, was more forthcoming. "We had limited e-mail contact after Jennifer made her accusations, but she has refused to ever meet with us under any conditions," Pamela Freyd told me when I reached her at FMSF headquarters in Philadelphia, where—fifteen years after cofounding the organization—she continues to maintain regular office hours, answering the phones that still ring, Monday through Thursday, 9 A.M. to 4 P.M.

"It's difficult to describe the shock, the horror, the devastation, the emptiness of learning about the accusation," Pamela said. "I've done my best to put it in the back of my mind."

"If your husband didn't molest your daughter," I asked, "why do you think she accused him?"

"She was in a period of extreme emotional distress," Pamela answered. "Sadly, after the reading I've done, I believe most accusations were designed to deliver the maximum pain. They were delivered at holidays, birthdays, out of the blue. One of the 'survivor' books suggests this."

Pamela didn't need to say which survivor book she was talking about. It was *The Courage to Heal*, of course.

"The false memory phenomenon was a disaster waiting to happen," she said. "It was a runaway movement, and it happened to tens of thousands of families. There are still people in jail who were convicted on 'recovered memory' testimony."

Since its founding in 1992, she told me, twenty-five thousand families had contacted the FMSF.

"Professionals who should have known better were just as vulnerable to unscientific ideas as the general public. This phenomenon demonstrated how good intentions can go so far astray when they're ruled by emotion rather than by reason."

Pamela's tone was dispassionate, suddenly; she sounded more like the Ph.D. she was than the loving mother she said she wanted another chance to be. "This whole phenomenon is a fascinating example of how unscientific beliefs can take hold and do great harm when people panic—just like when people panic in a fire.

"The underlying belief in 'repression' remains in our society," she concluded. "Until more scientific ideas about memory are a part of the training of every mental health worker, we won't be able to prevent this from arising again."

The Palm Beach Post
March 1, 2008
"Headmaster's Evil Lives on in
20-Year-Old Abuse Case"

Stuart—Little children, lots of little children, were raped and defiled in unspeakable ways by a man some of the smartest and richest people in the community had trusted to care for their sons and daughters.

It was March 1, 1988, when Stuart Detective Peggy Schwarz and state attorney's investigator Larry Lawson arrested Glendale Montessori owner James Toward on charges of sexual battery on a child, lewd and lascivious assault on a child and kidnapping. Investigators later learned of up to 60 victims, most ages 2 to 5.

Toward, now 77, pleaded guilty to molesting or kidnapping the [children] and was sentenced to 27 years in prison. Toward is challenging his commitment and maintains his innocence, saying his plea was only to avoid a harsher sentence.

—*Jill Taylor*

In the small town of Stuart, Florida, a twenty-year-old McMartinesque preschool case was heating up all over again.

As if time had stood still, the FMSF was at the center of the storm.

Supporters of James Toward, including a former Glendale student, set up a Web site, freejamestoward.com, "Dedicated to voicing truth and unraveling the mystery surrounding the incarceration of an innocent man: James Toward."

FMS Foundation Newsletter
Spring 2008
Vol. 17, No. 2

In February 2008, a former student at the Glendale Montessori School contacted the Foundation. She explained that when she was 9 years old, she had been sent to a therapist who used hypnosis to try to uncover her "memories" of being abused at Glendale when she was two, three and four. . . .

The former Glendale student said that after a lot of investigation, she is now certain that Toward had been wrongly convicted, and she wants to find a way to free James Toward.

Evidence of the beliefs that were circulating in the community (and thus the reason for using hypnosis on the former student), can be seen in the following quote that appeared in a 1992 article of the *Palm Beach Post*.

"Therapists say many victims [of Glendale Montessori] have blocked any memory of what happened to them at Glendale, possibly because they were told terrible things would happen if they remembered."

freejamestoward.com
"A Glendale Parent Speaks Out"

James . . . I wish you good luck in your hearing. . . . I remember only too well the panic of the times, and the way in which so many of us (parents) were caught up in the horror of it all.

It was impossible to know whether what we were hearing was real, or not. . . . I was reading the same books, knew all about what was going on across the country, and found myself in a state of suspended disbelief. . . .

It was the worst of times. The rumor and innuendo that circulated was insane. Gossip and speculation presented as truth. Many of us behaved as if we were completely mad. We withdrew our children from Camp High Rocks in the Carolinas because it was represented that "the Cult" was reprogramming our children while they were there!

I know of two parents who actually went out under cover of darkness to keep watch on [another parent's] home because they were convinced that members of a Satanic Cult were visiting her on nights of the full moon!

One parent actually "bugged" a local nursery school, hoping to catch the teachers in the act of molesting children. Another parent dug up the grounds at the school, looking for tunnels and hidden graves. . . . [T]he nagging reality in the back of my mind was always there: "But, we were DROP-IN PARENTS, always showing up at the school, unannounced, day in/day out!"

It was a time of total insanity, and though there are few of us who maintain contact today, only too happy to let those times fade into obscurity, I often wonder how many there are who, like me, feel that it was all some sort of mass hysteria that infected our community even as examples of the same happened all over the country. . . .

I don't know what purpose this letter will serve, other than to let you know that there's at least one person who supports the probability that you are, indeed, completely innocent.

I suppose I want you to know how sad I feel for your wife and daughter, and for you and the years you have lost. And, indeed for all the rest of us, who got caught up in it, despite ourselves, and who—however unwittingly—contributed to what happened to you.

Shortly after that anonymous letter was posted on James Toward's Web site, I was put in touch with the woman who wrote it. When I reached her at her law office in Stuart, Florida, she lowered her voice and asked me to call her "Margaret."

"I'd like to use my real name in your book, and in the letter I posted on James's Web site," she said. "But my business partners asked me not to. We have clients who are former Glendale parents. They won't do business with us if they find out that I'm trying to get James out of jail."

"Is the town still that polarized, twenty years later?" I asked.

"You have no idea," she answered without hesitation. She sighed. "I've never been able to rid myself of the poison of that time. It went through us like wildfire, this panic. It was Salem all over again."

In 1980, Margaret told me, she'd arrived with her husband and two toddlers in Stuart: population fifteen thousand, Sailfish Capital of the World. "Our neighbors raved about Glendale Montessori School, so we sent Sam and Nathan there," Margaret said. "I stopped in unannounced several times a week. I saw for myself that my children were doing just fine."

Her older son, Nathan, formed a special bond with the school's director, a lean, lanky Brit expat named James Toward. "Mr. T spent hours teaching Nathan to use the abacus." Margaret's voice swelled with emotion. "Nate's a brilliant architect now, thanks in large part to James Toward."

In 1988, two years after her sons had moved on to public school, Margaret got a call from the same neighbor who'd recommended Glendale Montessori. "She'd had her kids evaluated by a therapist," Margaret said. "He'd told her that every child who'd ever gone to that school had likely been abused."

Margaret was skeptical, but she did her due diligence. "I started calling other parents. The first father I spoke with was absolutely beside himself. He'd sent his kids to a psychologist who'd said they manifested 'precocious sexuality' they must have learned from whatever had happened at Glendale."

When James Toward was arrested, he plea-bargained to keep his staff members, including his wife, from being indicted, and to avoid what appeared to be a certain life sentence if the case went to trial. Glendale's thirty-year-old office manager, Brenda

Williams, was also arrested. She was convicted and sentenced to ten years in prison.

"The whole town went with the notion that where there's smoke, there's fire," Margaret told me. "Suddenly the local paper was saturated with horror stories about the atrocities Mr. T had supposedly committed.

"I didn't want to be a negligent parent. I took my kids to the psychiatrist who was treating the other kids. Dr. Miller regressed my boys and pronounced Nate 'iffy.' He told Nate that sometimes brains forget things that are too upsetting to remember.

"The poor kid was scared witless. He was desperate to come up with whatever it was he was supposed to remember. It was clear to me the therapy was doing more harm than good, so I decided to conduct my own investigation.

"The detective in charge of the case was also Sam's soccer coach." Margaret lowered her voice. "She let me spend three days in her office going through boxes and boxes of files, including the interviews with the six boys who'd filed the original charges.

"By the way," Margaret said, "one of those six was the son of Dr. Miller's receptionist. Another was the child of a prominent developer in town.

"What I found in the boxes was a whole bunch of nothing. No animal sacrifices, no blood, no oral sex, no sodomy. Nothing to indicate porn. That brought me to my senses. I decided: no more.

"I managed to yank my kids out of therapy before they got too damaged," Margaret added, "but the panic that was sweeping Stuart was impossible to avoid. I felt peer-pressured to attend the support group that met in a local dentist's office. Every Tuesday night the parents sat in a circle, swapping stories of satanic ritual abuse that their kids were bringing home from their therapy sessions.

"One father, a self-appointed 'satanist vigilante,' came to meetings packing a gun and sat there with his hand in his pocket," Margaret recalled. "The man who'd organized the group was distributing 'Believe the Children' bumper stickers and paraphernalia. It was mayhem.

"The therapists insisted the children they'd counseled would require therapy for the rest of their lives. The DA said he had enough evidence to prosecute.

"The FBI came in to investigate and issued a report denouncing the whole satanic conspiracy theory. Their report was roundly rejected by the townspeople, who decided the FBI must be in on the conspiracy. Anyone who defended James, including me, was labeled a satanist."

"Incredible," I said.

"But true," Margaret countered. "And bear in mind: most of those parents had master's degrees. We were a Montessori community; bright, thinking, intelligent people."

Stuart, 2010; Salem, 1692, I thought. "They still believe that James Toward did those things to their kids?"

Margaret laughed hollowly. "I'll never know. I think the agreement they made with the insurance company stipulates that they're not to speak of it, ever again."

"What insurance company?" I asked.

"Glendale was insured against claims like these," Margaret answered. "Persecuting James Toward became a very profitable enterprise. It still is. The parents sued the school and got huge settlements from the school's insurance company.

"The therapists made a fortune 'treating' the children, then serving as expert witnesses in the lawsuits. The lawyers didn't do too badly, either. Twenty years later, some of the students are still getting five thousand dollars a month under the terms of the civil suits."

I thought of all the American towns like Stuart, Florida, in which day-care workers like James Toward had been falsely accused of abusing children. I thought of the journalistic imperative to follow the money. Most injustices benefit *someone*—in this case, a town full of someones.

I wondered how many millions of dollars had changed hands—were continuing to change hands—in what had been portrayed as a psychologically driven case of mass panic, but was clearly driven by greed as well.

When Margaret spoke again, her voice was choked. "It never occurred to me that James would be in prison his entire life, effectively gone and forgotten by the players in this particular drama.

"One brave student came forward to say she'd been manipulated by her therapist when she was sent to him at age ten. That student now believes that her so-called memories were false. She's working with James's wife, trying to get him out. But not one other Glendale student has been heard from. Even my own sons want to leave the past in the past. And believe me, *they're* not being paid for their silence."

Margaret sighed again. "The Glendale kids are in their twenties and thirties now. I'm thinking of getting on Facebook, trying to chase some of them down. But I need to do it in a way that won't rattle too many cages and make them close ranks against the truth, the way they did twenty years ago.

"I'm going to the prison to visit James tomorrow morning. Maybe he'll have some ideas."

Freetoward.org
June 2008
"A Letter from James"

Dear Reader,

Incalculable harm has been done to a "small" number of members of a small community, in a small county, in Florida. Lives have been blighted, relationships destroyed, marriages torn asunder, children's faith in themselves shattered, their parents and society damaged. . . .

To them I say, rebuild those damaged areas of your personalities; curiosity, delight in learning, the buoyancy and love of life, the readiness to be friendly—make friends. Yes, be friendly and make friends, learn to trust because that was the stage in your development that was broken.

There is no shame or disgrace attached to you, because they belong to the adults who tried to put them on you. They tried to convince you that you were damaged **when you were not**; you were a whole, good person in the making when last I saw you. Go ahead, it is not too late, you are still young and have your life ahead of you to complete your healing!

"There is no crueler tyranny than that which is perpetrated under the shield of law and in the name of justice."—Charles de Montesquieu, 1742

—James H. Toward, No. 990114,
Florida Civil Commitment Center

The person who introduced me to Margaret also arranged for me to call James Toward at the Florida Civil Commitment Center.

"If you didn't abuse all those kids," I asked him, "why did you plead guilty?"

Not exactly a friendly question, but the circumstances didn't allow for niceties. The periodic beeping in my ear reminded me that the prison guards were monitoring our telephone conversation and could end it at any time.

I expected Toward to bristle. He laughed. "I realize that's the logical question to ask me," he said. "But it was so easy to decide to take the plea.

"Two years after I was arrested, while I was still in jail awaiting trial, the DA issued warrants for my wife and two of our teachers.

"I knew it was a ploy to make me accept the guilty plea, which I'd already rejected three times. But our daughter was fourteen years old. After all she'd been through, I couldn't leave her motherless."

In other words, I thought, *if he's telling the truth, James Toward pled guilty to abusing dozens of children in order to protect his own.*

Big if.

"The whole time I've been incarcerated, I've been prepared to leave here at a moment's notice," Toward continued in an ironic, wry tone that belied the situation he was describing. "Now I'm in a lockdown institution. They're telling me that if I'll just confess to the crimes for which I'm incarcerated—none of which I committed—I'll be eligible for a sex offender treatment program instead."

He chuckled. "How do you like the inanity of that?"

Is he joking because he's the sociopath his townspeople make him out to be? Or because he's so grounded in his own truth that their version can't shake his?

"It's been quite the roller coaster ride. One of my motions after another has been denied. Roller coasters can be fun . . ." That smile in his voice again. "But not at these prices."

"You're in prison for a crime you say you didn't commit," I blurted. "How can you be making *jokes?*"

"You've heard that saying, 'Do or die'?" Toward replied. "Well, I don't want to die. I'm here, but I don't have to sit in the corner and weep. My lawyer and I are preparing for a new trial. My hope is that this one will be the end of the line and the beginning of a new life."

"I heard that you meditate every day," I said.

"I plead guilty."

"And you're a facilitator in the prison's anger management program?"

"Guilty as charged."

"How do you manage your *own* anger?"

"I shall be seventy-nine years old this year," Toward told me, his British inflection deepening with emotion. "I believe I'll be set free to pursue a new and fruitful life with my family—as far from any roller coaster as I can get."

I found myself laughing along with him. How strange was this? I'd made this phone call expecting a grim interview with a defensive accused child molester. But I was starting to like the guy. *Is it a trick? Am I falling for another Big Lie?*

"You're such a good listener, I hate to leave you," Toward said—sincerely, my gut told me—"but they're serving a meal."

He paused for comedic effect. "There's only one dinner seating at this restaurant. If I don't make this one, I'll go hungry."

"Maybe you should take your business elsewhere," I joked along with him.

"I'll look into that." Toward turned serious. "Meredith. Thank you so much for caring about my situation."

Who said anything about caring? I'm interviewing you.

"You're welcome," I said, and then I realized that he was right. I did believe that James Toward was innocent, and I did care what happened to him.

How had I decided that so quickly—as quickly as I'd decided fifteen years ago that Gary Ramona was guilty?

The TC Palm
January 23, 2009
"Trial for Convicted Child Molester Who Ran Glendale Montessori School Slated for April"

Stuart—A leg-shackled and handcuffed James Toward shuffled into court Friday. . . . The jury could find he should be confined indefinitely in order to receive sexual offender treatment.

In July 1999, as he was about to be paroled, officials ordered him held at a treatment center for sex offenders after state psychiatrists concluded there was a 1-in-5 chance he would molest again.

"This was an era where this was going on all over the country," [Toward's defense attorney, Rusty Akins] said. "Because of the interview techniques, the entire way a child was interviewed was changed after that."

"It wasn't really false testimony by the children," he added. "It was suggested testimony by the children, what they call implanted memory."

More than a dozen parents came forward with allegations Toward had sexually abused their children.

Toward though, still maintains his innocence. Akins described his client as an "intelligent, articulate" man with failing health.

—*Melissa E. Holsman*

The TC Palm
January 23, 2009
"Responses to 'Trial for [James Toward], Convicted Child Molester'"

Oldladyintheshoe writes: As a mother whose child was a victim of this animal, it sickens me to think he is still tying up our court system. I want to vomit at the mere mention of his name. The only justice and peace of mind I get when I think of that animal is the treatment I pray he received from his fellow cell mate.

OscarRomero writes: I remember this case. I share your righteous fury. This slime has no right to live another second. I feel sympathy for the convicts that are forced to share space with this wicked demon! Sometimes I think justice would be served if a vigilante reached out and helped society by disposing of such filth. God have Mercy on the children.

MocoLoco writes: Justice is never served by vigilanteism [sic]. We as a nation need to amend the constitution to more clearly define cruel and unusual punishment and specify that murderers, rapists, and child molesters MUST be executed, thus taking these decisions out of the hands of the Supreme Court.

OscarRomero writes: A vigilante is a person who violates the law in order to exact what they believe to be justice from criminals, because they think that the criminal will not be caught or will not be sufficiently punished by the legal system. It is perfectly moral for injured parties to take action when the system has failed. Taking the life of a monster like this should be encouraged.

thirteen

In Neuroscience We Trust

If I were in a community in which everyone
believed they'd been molested, my brain would
reorganize my memory to match that belief.
Eventually my memory would be physiologically
embedded with a sense of certainty. My brain
would reward and reinforce that feeling because
the sensation of absolute certainty lights up the
pleasure center of the brain—like heroin, or sex.
—*Robert Burton, former chief of neurology,*
Mt. Zion-UCSF Hospital.
Interview with the author,
September 2008

Much had changed, psychology-wise, since thousands of us
marched lockstep into incest therapists' offices and incest workshops and incest support groups with the same story on our
outraged lips.

Twenty years later, brain chemistry, not childhood, was the
manna of mental health; pharmaceuticals, not talk therapy, had
been anointed the miracle cure. Neuroscientists, not psycho-
therapists, were the mind gurus du jour. The scene of the action
had shifted from the therapists' offices to basement university
neuroscience labs, where researchers slid sedated subjects head-
first into the clanging maws of MRI machines.

If you can't beat 'em, interview 'em is my motto. So I decided to talk to some brain scientists, starting with neurologist Robert Burton. Author of the mind-science column on Salon.com, Burton's 2008 book, *On Being Certain: Believing You Are Right Even When You're Not*, explores the part that brain physiology plays in developing a sense of certainty.

I briefed him on my story. "So," he said, "you got caught up in the flying-saucer mass hysteria of the 1980s."

I started to protest—"We weren't *that* stupid," and then said yes instead.

"Are you sure now that you were wrong?" Burton asked.

I considered this. "I don't know if I'll ever be completely sure of anything again," I said. "But I'm as sure as I can be."

"Understandable," Burton said.

"So tell me," I asked. "How could so many of us have been so sure we were right when we were so wrong?"

"Certainty is a combo platter of biology, genetics, early child-hood experience, and environment," Burton answered. "It starts as a psychological phenomenon and then becomes biological. Our ability to change a strongly held belief depends on how deeply rooted the neural networks are."

I thought about Jim Carrey having his memories erased in the 2004 movie *Eternal Sunshine of the Spotless Mind*.

"If I'd come to you twenty years ago and stuck my head into your MRI machine," I asked, "could you have told me whether my accusation was true or false?"

"*f*MRI," Burton corrected me. He told me that in 1992, the MRI had been replaced by the functional MRI, which records dynamic images instead of static snapshots, showing changes in the flow of oxygenated blood to the brain. Changes in the oxygen level, he said, reflect the increased effort of telling a lie.

"Even if the technology had been capable of making that determination then—which it wasn't—a true believer wouldn't have been convinced.

"Certainty can only be dispelled by overwhelming contrary evidence with an equal level of certainty. You were sure that your dad had molested you. Seeing your brain lighting up on a screen wouldn't have changed your mind."

As I was considering this, Burton added, with great certainty, "A false memory might start out as a psychological quirk, but it quickly becomes a physiological phenomenon."

So it wasn't all my fault, I thought. Like the mind reader he is, Burton commented, "Flying saucers or incest, it makes no difference. Feelings of absolute certainty and utter conviction aren't rational deliberate conclusions. They're involuntary mental sensations generated by the brain."

I liked Burton's explanation. I liked the out it offered me. "My neural pathways made me do it" had such a seductively self-righteous ring.

According to Burton, my memory had just been following orders. The same way my iPhone synchs to my computer, my brain had synched my memory to match the prevailing beliefs. My synapses made sparks fly with those yummy flashes of certainty, making me feel good. Like heroin, as the good doctor said. Like sex.

I won't lie. If I could have convinced myself that this explanation were true, my soul searching would have stopped there. But I know that I'm more than my biology. The reasons for my accusation ran deeper than the poor-me pathways that I, with much assistance from the culture, had etched into my own brain. It was the truth, the whole truth, and nothing but the truth I was after, and the synapse story didn't quite satisfy.

Absent the recovered-memory craze, would I have convinced myself that my father had molested me? Probably not.

But I'd lived fifty-seven years in the United States of Anything Goes, where one rationale for human misbehavior rises to the level of certainty, only to be debunked by the next.

Take a socially acceptable shortcut to redemption? Been there, tried that, paid the price. This time I'd be taking the long way home.

The New York Times
August 13, 2009
"False 'Death Panel' Rumor Has
Some Familiar Roots"

The stubborn yet false rumor that President Obama's health care proposals would create government-sponsored "death panels" to decide which patients were worthy of living seemed to arise from nowhere in recent weeks.

The assertion nonetheless seemed reminiscent of the modern-day viral Internet campaigns that dogged Mr. Obama last year, falsely calling him a Muslim and questioning his nationality.

. . . The specter of government-sponsored, forced euthanasia was raised . . . long before any legislation had been drafted, in an outlet with opinion pages decidedly opposed to Mr. Obama, *The Washington Times.*

In an editorial, the newspaper reminded its readers of the Aktion T4 program of Nazi Germany in which "children and adults with disabilities, and anyone anywhere in the Third Reich was subject to execution who was blind, deaf, senile, retarded, or had any significant neurological condition."

—*Jim Rutenberg and Jackie Calmes*

The University of California at Irvine—whose endless expansion inspired the rumor that UCI actually stands for "Under Construction Indefinitely"—houses one of the top-ranked behavioral neuroscience programs in the country.

The school has recruited a cluster of top memory researchers to make sure it stays that way.

One is James McGaugh, director of UCI's Center for the Neurobiology of Learning and Memory. McGaugh is also past president of the American Psychological Society, an American Academy of Arts and Sciences Fellow, and founding editor of the journal *Neurobiology of Learning and Memory*, among many other impressive CV items. One thing McGaugh is not, I soon learned, is wishy-washy.

"I do *not* believe there's such a thing as repressed memory," McGaugh told me. "I haven't seen a single instance in which a memory was completely repressed and popped up again.

"I go on science, not fads. And there's absolutely no proof that it can happen. Zero. None. Niente. Nada. All my research says that strong emotional experiences leave emotionally strong memories. Being sexually molested would certainly qualify."

I asked him to explain how that happens, neuroscientifically speaking.

"When we get emotionally aroused about something really important," McGaugh answered, "we release stress hormones—adrenaline, cortisol—into the bloodstream. Those hormones activate the region of the brain called the amygdala, which releases a neurotransmitter called norepinephrine. You with me so far?"

"So far," I said, wishing I'd paid more attention—any attention—in my high school science class. Too bad my amygdala had been so focused on my sexy boyfriend and that pesky Vietnam War.

"The amygdala communicates with the areas of the brain where memories are being formed, and tells the brain to make a strong memory. I've done hundreds of experiments to validate this.

"The stronger the memory, the less likely it is to be turned into a false memory. You remember your fifth-grade teacher, don't you?"

How could I forget the terrifying Mrs. Levy? "All too well."

"I might be able to convince you that she was your sixth-grade teacher. But I'd never convince you that she was your college professor."

Especially because I never quite made it to college, I thought, but I got his point.

I asked McGaugh if he was familiar with the false-memory panic of the 1980s. "Absolutely," he answered with characteristic equivocation. "Holly Ramona was an undergraduate here before she made those fantastic claims against her father, so I followed the case."

I could practically hear him shaking his head in disgust. "There are always psychological fads going around, but that was an era of profound therapeutic malfeasance. And greed."

"Greed?"

"Suddenly it's fashionable for a young man to say he was molested by a Catholic priest. Some of them are thinking, 'There's money to be made here.'"

"When I accused my dad of molesting me," I said, "I wasn't motivated by therapeutic malfeasance. Or greed."

"On what evidence did you base your claim?" McGaugh asked.

"I was having these dreams—"

I didn't know a person could actually *harrumph*, but that's what McGaugh did. "Dreams don't mean a damn thing to me."

"I had flashbacks, too."

"Believing that flashbacks represent memories of actual experiences is like believing in fairies—which a lot of people do. As a famous person said, 'You're entitled to your own opinion, but not your own facts.'

"The majority of people in this country don't believe in evolution. Think about that for a moment." McGaugh paused for dramatic effect.

"And what about those people who claim that Obama's not a citizen, Obama's a Muslim, Obama's health care plan will kill old people? They let their values create the facts for them.

"I'm a scientist," McGaugh concluded. "I don't go on beliefs. I go on verifiable facts."

Goddess knows I had ample evidence that my beliefs weren't foolproof. But I wouldn't have wanted to live without them nonetheless. Although I agreed with McGaugh's analysis of the "birthers" and "teabaggers" who transposed values and facts and truth and lies, McGaugh's world seemed to me utterly fact based, and terribly cold.

"You really should talk to a colleague of mine," McGaugh advised me. "Recovered memory is Elizabeth Loftus's specialty."

I attempted to repress a shudder, but the memories were too strong. In 2002, Elizabeth Loftus was rated the top-ranked woman among the one hundred most influential researchers in psychology in the twentieth century. And during the 1980s and early 1990s, Loftus was number one on my Ten Most Unwanted List. Front woman for the FMSF, "The Diva of Disclosure" had been an expert witness in hundreds of recovered-memory cases, including Gary Ramona's. Her defense of accused fathers had made her such a lightning rod that she'd had to hire bodyguards to protect herself.

I was striving to evolve beyond the Balkanization of the past, looking for truth, not validation of the us-versus-them views I'd once held dear. But—talk to Elizabeth Loftus? I wasn't sure that I was past the past enough to do *that*.

More Magazine
September 2009
"The Childhood She Couldn't Remember"

It wasn't until I was in my late twenties that I sought help for the depression and inexplicable anger I'd felt all my life. . . .

> With the encouragement of a counselor, I asked my mother if something had happened to me when I was young, something I should remember but didn't. That's when she told me about the night my uncle, who was living with us, crept into my bed and raped me.
>
> ... In my late thirties, I finally accepted that the rape had happened, even though I still could not remember it.
>
> —*Beatriz Terrazas*

A scope's throw from James McGaugh's headquarters in the School of Biological Sciences, Dr. Michael Rugg and his team toil in UCI's fNiM (functional Neuro-imaging of Memory) Lab, using fMRI technology to "investigate the cognitive and neural bases of memory encoding and retrieval."

I explained my involvement in the recovered-memory panic, and asked Rugg if his research could help explain what had happened to me and my fellow retractors.

"There's extensive work demonstrating how relatively easy it is to fool the memory system into retrieving a memory of an event that never happened," Rugg said.

"When we retrieve a memory, it's not like winding a video back and replaying it. The information we recover is blended with one's current situation, biases, and cognitive states to produce what we experience as a memory. Every time we retrieve a memory we reencode it."

"How?" I asked.

"We don't know all the different ways the brain stores memory. But we believe that the efficacy with which one neuron stimulates another is an important factor. Neurons communicate with each other through little gaps called synapses. Synaptic strength is what produces memory."

"I've never thought of memory as being so . . . anatomical."

Rugg laughed. "There's no distinction between physiological and emotional memories."

"What about conscience?" I asked. "What about the *soul?*"

"The soul is a completely unnecessary concept for explaining how the brain works," Rugg answered. "From a strictly scientific point of view, I don't need to know if a rat has a soul to explain its behavior.

"You know that old saying: if you repeat a lie long enough and often enough, you'll end up with a significant number of people believing it. The headlines are full of that sort of thing."

Unlike McGaugh, Rugg was slow talking, pensive. Also unlike McGaugh, Rugg believes that strong emotions are more likely to distort memories than to strengthen them.

"A great deal of research shows that the confidence someone has in a memory can be completely disconnected from the accuracy of that memory," he said. "Especially emotionally arousing memories, like those of childhood sexual abuse.

"The way we typically judge whether a memory is real is the confidence and the vividness with which we're able to construct it. But memories don't get retrieved with little flags on them saying, 'This may not be right.'"

"What about dreams?" I said. "I had so many dreams of being an incest survivor."

"It would be a brave person who thought he or she understood what determines the content of dreams," Rugg said. "Some believe that dreaming is some kind of residue of thoughts you had during the day. If you dreamed about being abused, that just means you were thinking about it. It doesn't mean it happened. You can dream about a unicorn, too, but there are no unicorns— except in your head."

"Careful," I teased him. "You're talking about my favorite place to be."

We shared a chuckle, and I realized that I live in a very different world from McGaugh and Rugg's. In my writer's

world, everything is possible. In their scientists' world, only
the provable is possible. Where, I wondered, do our universes
overlap?

I asked Rugg about the impact on memory of being surrounded by people who were constructing similar memories.
Bingo: the confluence of science and the imagination.

"Knowing that others are having these experiences," he said,
"may well play into mental state. If someone's being bombarded
by a particular phenomenon like recovered memory, that pro-
vides the context in which memories get interpreted.

"That context, in turn, creates a schema—an organizational
framework the mind uses to interpret thoughts, memories, per-
ceptions, and the like."

It all sounds so *neutral*, I mulled aloud. No right or wrong,
no blame, no accountability. Just neurons and synapses, doing
what they were designed to do.

"Science has nothing to say about morality," Rugg said. "But
I happen to think it's extremely important to hold people responsible for their actions and the consequences that follow."

"So much for letting me off the hook," I grumbled.

"One application of scientific evidence is to help people
understand why they do what they do." Rugg was silent for a
moment, and then he added, "You might want to talk to my
colleague, Elizabeth Loftus. She'd have more to say about your
. . . dilemma."

"Thanks for the tip," I said.

I expected Elizabeth Loftus to check me out, blow my cover, then
blow off my interview request. But my longtime archenemy
proved surprisingly available. And surprisingly thoughtful. And
surprisingly *human*.

"The memory war was the major mental health scandal of
the twentieth century," Loftus said. "And it's not over. Last week
I was in Wisconsin, testifying for a seventy-eight-year-old grand-

father whose adult niece suddenly 'remembered' that he'd molested her.

"We exported it to other countries, too," Loftus continued. "I've been a consultant in recovered-memory cases in Ireland, Portugal, New Zealand, and Sweden. I just came back from Switzerland. It looks like things are heating up there, too."

Was it my (biased) imagination, or did this *excite* her? "How did you become the Diva of Disclosure?" I asked.

"I've been an expert on memory since the mid-seventies," Loftus answered. "But I didn't get into the memory war business until I consulted on a recovered-memory trial in 1990.

"In those days all the talk shows were having survivors on to tell their stories, bathing them in a love bath of empathy, giving them a whole new identity and a lot of rewards based on their survivor status. Oprah and 60 *Minutes* or whoever would trot me out as a skeptical opinion.

"Later, I got angrier. The repression aficionados kept trying to salvage their theories. Meanwhile I saw the destruction of families. The Ramona trial was a turning point—"

"I went to that trial," I interjected. "I wrote about it."

"I would have bet my house that Gary Ramona was innocent," Loftus said.

"I would have bet my house *and* yours that he was guilty," I said.

The phone line hummed. Then we both laughed. And then I came clean and told Loftus my "retractor story."

"Who were you a victim of, that you caused such pain for people around you?" Loftus asked me. "Retractors are victims too, you know."

"I wasn't victimized," I said. And then, sarcastically: "But I'm open to suggestion."

"Sounds like you *were* rather suggestible," Loftus said. "After what you've been through, I'd be surprised if you're still as gullible as you once were."

"I'm not sure that's true," I said.

Loftus snickered. "You just proved my point."

"Seriously," she continued, "people always look for an explanation for their dysfunctional thoughts, feelings, and behaviors. Retractors like you came up with a good one. A colleague of mine called it 'A-B-C':

"C: you're *crazy*. No one likes that explanation for their behavior, so they go on to B.

"B: you're a *bad* person. No one wants that, either.

"A: you were *abused*, so nothing is your fault. Needless to say, that's the most popular explanation."

"Not for me," I said, feeling just a smidge defensive. "I'm actually trying to figure out why I did it. Why *we* did it."

"Do you still believe in repressed memory?" Loftus asked.

"I only know enough to know that I don't know."

"When I wrote my first article on repressed memories in 1993," Loftus said, "I was still thinking maybe there was such a thing. But it struck me as strange that most traumas produce precisely the opposite problem—intrusive memories.

"Now I'm totally convinced. There's no scientific evidence for the theory of repression.

"I mean, *please*." Loftus' voice vibrated with indignation. "Holly Ramona was raped from age five to age sixteen, forced to have sex with the family dog—and all of that is banished to her unconscious till she's eighteen and goes into therapy?" Loftus snorted. "Where's the proof that memory ever works that way?"

"What about Jennifer Freyd's theory of betrayal trauma?" I asked, knowing that Loftus was firmly entrenched on the elder Freyds' side of the memory wars, and was therefore likely to be at war with their daughter.

"I can't tell you what happened in Jennifer's situation," Loftus said, "but I don't think she repressed and recovered it. Jennifer has gotten a lot of rewards for being a sex-abuse survivor. It's her whole career now."

Two decades of demonizing Loftus were back in a flash. "Jennifer has a career as a memory researcher, not as an incest survivor," I said. "She wouldn't talk about her family, and I begged."

"Well, she hasn't done anything to prove repression exists," Loftus retorted. "*Nothing*. All she has is a theory."

I felt a flush of the old antagonism. Why did I care what Elizabeth Loftus thought of Jennifer Freyd? Because I was still attached to my us-versus-them, 1980s point of view? Because I believed Jennifer—instinctively, the way I believed Holly Ramona? Because being in the middle of a conflict made it hard to avoid choosing sides?

"Do you consider yourself a feminist?" I asked, sounding snippy, even to myself.

"I'm an equity feminist. I believe in equal pay for equal work." Unlike me, Loftus sounded utterly unruffled. "I've had opportunities because women before me opened doors. But sometimes the word 'feminist' conjures up man bashing, blaming women's oppression on men. I'm not one of those."

Looking for common ground, I asked if Loftus had any regrets about her part in the memory wars.

"None," she answered without hesitation. "It's been very gratifying to be able to apply my science to the real world. Although I did go through a low period when they turned on me and started making my life miserable."

So retractors weren't the only ones who thought the para-noiacs were out to get us? "Who's 'they'?" I asked.

"Recovered-memory therapists, people who still think they're survivors, some of their supporters. They drummed up a letter-writing campaign to the chair of my department at my former university. That played a role in my leaving a job I'd had for twenty-nine years.

"I also spent four years in litigation with a recovered-memory lady who sued me. I'll tell you this: it's much more fun being an expert consultant to litigation than being a party to it."

"I'm sure that's true."

Loftus hesitated. "Did you take your dad to court?"

"No."

"Thank God for that, at least."

"I'm not sure who to thank," I demurred. "But I'm glad I didn't take my dad to court."

"Oops. I'm late for a meeting," Loftus said. "But I've really enjoyed this conversation."

"Much to my surprise," I confessed, "so have I."

fourteen

Amends

Oprah Winfrey: He was my favorite uncle. I was
just a little girl looking for attention and love. I
know now that abusers are manipulative human
beings. They seek out the little girls and boys who
are seeking love.

Kathryn Harrison, author of *The Kiss*, a memoir
of her four-year sexual relationship with her father:
"I invented a father who didn't exist. . . . My idea
of him was so powerful I didn't notice who he was.
I found out how far down I could go trying to
please other people. I was easily manipulated."
                            —*"Shattering the Secrecy of Incest,"*
                                    Oprah, *October 15, 2009*

Lucky me. Unlike true incest survivors, I wasn't sexually abused
by my father.

And lucky me. Unlike many retractors, when I came to my
senses my father was still alive and relatively well. I still had time
to made amends. But my family had been avoiding the subject
for a decade. If they'd wanted to talk about it, wouldn't we have
had that conversation by now?

"What's in it for me?" any and all of them might have
rightly asked.

An apology? That and a BART ticket would get them on
the subway.

Redemption? They weren't the ones who needed redeeming; that would be me.

But I had to try to right the wrong I'd done. Or, at least, explain what I knew about my false accusation that I hadn't known when I made it.

I took the first step and called my brother—least scary conversation first—and asked him to have lunch with me.

Doug and I met at a falafel joint near his house. The waiter filled our water glasses and said he'd be back to take our orders. *I'll have the forgiveness*, I thought. *With a side of insight.*

"You want to share the Meza plate?" Doug asked me.

"Sure," I said. "Doug. Do you remember the night I told you Dad had molested me?"

Doug glanced at me and then beckoned to the waiter, who came and took our order.

"I'm going to try to convince Dad to talk to me about it while he still can," I said.

"Good luck with that," my brother said. Neither of us had ever had much success dragging our father into a conversation he didn't want to have.

"I need to hear what you and the kids think about it," I said, "before I try to talk to him."

Doug dipped a pita triangle into a small red bowl of hummus, his forehead furrowed in thought. "At first I was in shock," he said. "Intuitively, I couldn't believe it. But it didn't seem possible that you were making it up."

Even as a toddler, my brother only said what he knew to be true. At age five, he'd issue driving directions from the backseat of the family DeSoto. "That kid's never wrong," my father used to say. *Unlike his sister*, he didn't have to add.

"I thought you were wrong to go public with your accusation," my brother continued. "And it was heartbreaking for Dad to be estranged from you. But I also knew that we both had pretty bad relationships with our father. So whether it was true or not, it was clear to me that you felt really wounded. And I understood why you did."

He took a sip of water. "Actually," he said, "I was sort of hoping you were right."

"*What?*"

"I've always felt like a mirror with Dad's reflection in it. If he was a child molester, that would have broken the mirror.

"I don't think I ever told you this," Doug added, "but after you accused Dad, I went to therapy to figure out if he'd molested me, too."

"You *did?*"

He nodded. "The therapist said I showed signs of PTSD, but I decided it hadn't happened. So I stopped seeing her."

The waiter set a platter of Levant sandwiches and dolmas and tabouli in the center of the table. "For me," my brother said, "the worst part of the whole thing was that I got really

self-conscious about touching Emmy. I wanted to be physically affectionate with my daughter, the way Dad never was
with you. But once that word 'incest' was in the air, I couldn't
do it."

I felt sick. "I'm so sorry," I said. "For what I did to you. And
what I did to Emmy."

Doug shrugged. "Every family has its fucked-up moments.
This was one of our more fucked-up ones."

Our most *fucked-up one*, I thought. Apparently it wasn't just
incest that had multigenerational consequences. So did false
allegations of incest. Twenty years ago I'd scoured the country
in search of perpetrators. In this case, I'd found the perpetrator,
and it was me.

"What happened between you and Dad," my brother said,
"could only happen when there's anger and disconnection
between a parent and a child."

Doug forked tabouli onto his plate. "The way I think about
this episode is that it wasn't really about recovered memory, or
incest, or abuse," he said. "I think it was about your search for
happiness."

I looked at him, puzzled.

"The human species has a hard time achieving balance," he
said. "It's hard to achieve balance when you're unhappy. You
were unhappy. You were looking for balance. You thought
you'd find it by putting the pieces into place, by remembering
that you'd been abused. I can't blame you for looking for
happiness."

I'd always been the troublemaker in our family, my brother
the peacemaker. He covered for me when I snuck out to see my
boyfriends, begged my mother and me to stop when we were
screaming at each other, sat in his room alone when my father
and I were having one of our locked-door talks, comforted me
when I emerged swollen-eyed and raging.

"That's generous of you," I said, "but I think you're protecting
me again."

Doug shrugged. "Old family dynamics die hard."

"What an optimist you are," I said. "I don't think they *ever* die."

Mackenzie Phillips was everywhere, promoting her book, sharing her incest story on every major media outlet, including several appearances on *Oprah*.

"Is she lying?" people asked in grocery store lines and blog posts. "Is incest consensual if it starts when the daughter is an adult?"

> "This mental case has gotten [*sic*] 'clean' from drugs count-
> less times over the course of her life that it's extremely
> hard to believe a word that comes out of her mouth,"
> wrote "Peanuts" on the TV-watch Web site zap2it.com.
>
> "Peanuts . . . you're an asshole," argued "NYCDeb." "It
> doesn't cross your tiny mind that maybe she couldn't get
> off drugs because of all she's had to deal with?"
>
> "Mackenzie is such a brave sole [*sic*] for coming forward
> like this . . . good for Oprah for bringing light to sub-
> stance and sexual abuse," "Meow" agreed.
>
> "Goldy Locks" wrote, "Am I supposed to believe this? Does
> she want me to feel sorry for her? Will the truth set her
> free, or just disturb the rest of us?"

Controversial as Mackenzie Phillips's confessional was, it raised a conversation that had been silenced (again) for too many years.

ABCNews.com
September 25, 2009
"Mackenzie Phillips' Confession Inspires Others to Come Forward"

Former child star Mackenzie Phillips' candid confession about her purported decade-long sexual relationship with her singer-father,

John Phillips, has forced the uncomfortable issue of incest into the public limelight.

Since Phillips' public admission this week, the Rape, Abuse and Incest National Network (RAINN) has reported a 26 percent jump in its hotline calls and an 83 percent increase in traffic on its Web site. . . .

Two of John Phillips' former wives said Mackenzie Phillips is lying.

—*Mariecar Frias and Kate McCarthy*

Talk about your old family dynamics. My mother and I had only been working on our relationship for the past fifty years.

We'd made progress in the past decade, learning when to process our hair-trigger reactions to each other and, more important, when not to. Making new, good memories instead of endlessly masticating the old, bad ones. At my mom's request, I'd even gone to see her therapist with her.

Now that I was old enough to be a grandmother, I found less to resent and more to admire about my eighty-year-old tennis-playing, human-rights-advocating, Sierra Club–volunteering mother, who still pushed me to full speed to keep up with her—in life, and on our hikes in the Berkeley hills.

"Mom," I wheezed, breathing twice as hard as she was as we chugged up a hill in Tilden Park. "I've been thinking about when I accused Dad—"

"I don't want to talk about that," my mother interjected. "It's too painful."

"Maybe talking about it will make it *less* painful," I argued.

"I can't stand to listen to any more excuses about what you did to this family," my mother said.

My throat tightened, a familiar ache. "I don't want to make excuses," I said. "I want to apologize."

In silence we plodded toward the cattle guard that bisects the trail. My mother crossed it confidently, gracefully navigating the widely spaced metal slats. Once she was on the other side, I followed her route precisely, as usual. As usual I stumbled, trapping one foot between the slats. By the time I extricated myself, my mother was twenty paces ahead of me with her back to me. As usual.

I'd lived my whole life racing to catch up to my mother, certain that she didn't want to be caught. For the first time, now, I wondered if the distance between us was really all her doing.

Was my mom really trying to get away from me? Or was I the one who was holding myself back, holding on to my victim story?

RAINN released some disturbing statistics based on the U.S. Department of Justice's 2004 National Crime Victimization Survey.

15 percent of sexual assault and rape victims are under age twelve.

29 percent are ages twelve to seventeen.

44 percent are under age eighteen.

80 percent are under age thirty.

The highest-risk years are twelve to thirty-four.

Girls age sixteen to nineteen are four times more likely than the general population to be victims of rape, attempted rape, or sexual assault.

7 percent of girls in grades 5 to 8 and 12 percent of girls in grades 9 to 12 said they had been sexually abused.

3 percent of boys grades 5 to 8 and 5 percent of boys in grades 9 to 12 said they had been sexually abused.

The New York Times
October 9, 2009
"No More Suffering in Silence"

The arrest of Roman Polanski for his 1977 crime of plying a 13-year-old girl with Champagne and Quaaludes before raping and sodomizing her, and the revelation from Mackenzie Phillips that she had had a 10-year "consensual incestuous" relationship with her own father that she believes began when she was a teenager, raises the question: How pervasive is child sexual abuse and how often do these crimes go unreported?

According to a 2000 report by the Bureau of Justice Statistics, nearly 70 percent of all sexual assaults are committed against children.

... If up to 3 in 10 girls and 3 in 20 boys are still being assaulted, these are epidemic proportions. And, if most cases are never reported, it's a silent epidemic.

—*Charles M. Blow*

My thirty-year-old son, Matthew, didn't want to talk about my accusation, either.

Goddess knows he didn't get it from me, but Matthew's always been gifted at knowing the difference between his own needs and other people's. Maybe because his boundaries are so secure, he's a master of compromise. He offered to answer one or two questions by e-mail instead.

Being me, I sent Matthew five questions. Being Matthew, he answered the promised two.

Do you remember how I told you about my accusation?

"No, not really . . . just that we couldn't see Grandpa. I somehow remember that Grandpa did something inappropriate to Charlie and that's why we couldn't see him."

Do you think this episode affected your relationships with Emmy and Zach? With Grandpa and Gloria? With me?

"I would imagine it affected all of our relationships. I've always wondered why we weren't that close with Grandpa and I guess this is why. I feel a little deprived of a relationship with my only grandfather . . . but I also realize that things aren't so simple and there are other factors involved. Not being able to go to dim sum with Grandpa, Gloria, Emmy and Zach really was pretty whack."

Restraining the urge to point out that his relationship with Emmy, at least, didn't seem to have suffered much—they'd been roommates for the first two years after Matthew moved to Los Angeles, and they'd been close all their lives—I thanked Matthew for his candor, and made a date for dinner with Charlie.

In his twenty-nine years, I'd never known Charlie to miss a chance to plumb the depths: his, anyone else's, the world's. So I wasn't surprised when we met at the Chinese dive where I used to strap him into a booster seat and he wasted no time laying it on the line.

"The most fun times in my childhood," he said, "were hanging out at Grandpa and Granny Gloria's apartment with Matthew and Emmy and Zach. Having sleepovers. Watching horse races on TV."

I pushed noodles around on my plate, wondering if he also remembered that one of those fun times had ended with his grandfather throwing him down on the couch hard enough to make him cry.

"Then all of a sudden I had no grandfather," Charlie said. "And Matthew and I were split apart from our cousins, who were more like a brother and sister to us. And we never really got back together."

So much for giving my kids the kind of family I never had. "Go on," I said.

"It changed my worldview. It made me think that life has holes in it. People will be taken away from you. The best thing in the world, which is family, isn't safe from people messing it up."

I met my son's eyes, remembering the years when he wouldn't meet mine, or anyone's, wondering if his adolescence might have been less life threatening if his family had felt safer to him.

Charlie swallowed a mouthful of cashew chicken and wiped his full lips: my grandmother's lips, my father's, mine. Would Charlie be sitting here thirty years from now, apologizing to a child of his, or being apologized to by a child of his who had that same Maran mouth?

"I'm so sorry I punched holes in your family," I said. "I was afraid Grandpa would hurt you. I thought I was doing the right thing."

"It might have been the right thing for you," Charlie said. "But it definitely wasn't the right thing for us."

My brother's son, Zach, the baby of the family, was eight years old when I made my accusation. At twenty-eight, he was a grad student at Columbia. I e-mailed him the same questions I'd sent to Matthew. He answered them in a very different way.

"I do remember—vividly—that there was some sort of accusation," he wrote. "And that I had a hard time understanding why my aunt (who I liked very much) had said that my grandfather (who I liked very much as well) did something sexual/ inappropriate to her.

"I remember, in fact, cringing at the thought, and thinking that something must have been missing from the story. I really couldn't reconcile the issue in my head or heart.

"I absolutely think this affected my relationship with Matthew and Charlie. They didn't get to know the grandparents that I LOVED and ADORED. And, sadly, I remember thinking that they didn't get to be spoiled by them the way Emmy and I were.

"I never blamed Matthew or Charlie but unfortunately, I remember feeling bitter towards you, Mer, as things began to change and it became clear (I think . . . it is clear, right?) that the accusations were ultimately false.

"Grandpa never let on that he was affected by the situation (that's the kind of guy he is) but I remember feeling so bad that such a gentle and generous man could be accused of something so terrible (I still don't know what EXACTLY the accusations were)."

"I'm so proud of you for telling me the truth," I wrote to Zach. "And I hope I haven't hurt you more by asking."

An instant message appeared at the bottom of my screen. "Stuff like this doesn't just go away," Zach typed. "I think this is a great step in the healing process. Try not to beat yourself up."

"Who *should* I beat up, then?" I wrote back.

"Umm . . . How 'bout no one?" he wrote.

"I'm a New Yorker," I typed. "You live there. You should know. To New Yorkers it's not whether you win or lose. It's where you lay the blame."

"Ha, ha. Save the rest of your bad jokes for later. I gotta go to class."

"Will do."

"I love you, Mer."

"I love you too."

"I didn't like hearing that about my grandfather," Emmy told me when I called her at the Laurel Canyon house she shared with Matthew and their two cats, Cash and Cookie.

"I tried not to pay attention to the details. It was painful to know that Grandpa hurt you. It was just as painful to know that he was hurting because you put him in a very negative light. And I wondered why, if that was true for you, I was allowed to spend the night at Grandpa and Granny Gloria's house."

"Your mom and dad asked me a few times if I thought you'd be safe with him," I said.

"And you said yes?"

"I did."

Emmy paused. "Then what about Matthew and Charlie?"

I sighed. "I know. It makes no sense."

"I didn't like not being able to share my Grandpa and Granny experiences with my closest cousins," Emmy said. "I had so many good times with my grandparents. And I felt bad if I talked about it to Matthew and Charlie.

"I remember them hanging out with us after you decided not to hate Grandpa. It was so wonderful to have them back and all of us together again. But I felt like everyone was uncomfortable because there was so much unsaid. And so many missed times together."

A thick silence fell between us. I was holding my breath, trying not to cry.

"Also, for a while I worried that if Grandpa did that to you," Emmy said slowly, "my dad would do it to me."

Knife in my heart. Since the day she was born I'd wanted to be a great role model for this girl, the only girlchild in our family. I'd been determined to lend her strength and joy and courage. I knew that I'd done that. And I knew, too, that by chasing the truth of my childhood, I'd stolen a piece of hers.

"You know your dad loves you," I said. "You know he'd never hurt you that way."

"Then why didn't you know that about *your* dad?"

The usual explanations sprang to my lips. They tasted like excuses. They tasted like crap.

I couldn't stop my tears. "I'm so sorry, Em."

"I never would have brought this up if you hadn't," she said. "I forgive you, Mer."

"Thank you for saying that. But I don't know why you would."

"Whenever I screw up, you always tell me, 'You're bigger than your mistakes.'"

"You're a size zero," I sniffled. "You're not bigger than *anything*."

Emmy snorted. I heard the smile in her voice. "So are you going to take your own advice, or what?"

"What?" I said, and we both laughed. But I was crying when we hung up. I hoped the same wasn't true of her.

As a child I desperately wanted my feelings to matter, my words to carry weight, my stories to be believed. And then finally my parents took me seriously; the world took *us* seriously—but only when what I was saying, what we were saying, wasn't true.

Was it power we wanted? We were daughters of the 1950s; we had reason to want more of it than we had. But I didn't want that kind of power anymore.

"He pretends he's forgotten about it," Gloria said when I asked her if I should try again to apologize to my father. "But I know that's not true. He needs to put it to rest while he still can."

Gloria told me to show up at their apartment on Saturday afternoon. "Don't call first," she advised me. "Got it," I said. "Sneak attack."

A few days later, I stepped off the elevator and found my dad leaning out of his apartment door, waving at me anxiously, as if I might decide to visit one of his neighbors instead if he didn't flag me down first.

"You look funny," he said as I approached him. He looked me up and down. "Did you always dress like that?"

Why did I wear a clinging top to talk to my father about incest?

Am I going to be asking myself questions like this for the rest of my life?

"Oh, for God's sake, Stan," Gloria said from behind my dad. Shaking her head, she gave me a hug and pulled us into the living room.

"The strangest thing happened last night," my father told me. "Or was it this morning? I woke up at two o'clock. It was dark outside, and I thought it was the middle of the day."

"You're eighty-one years old, Dad," I said. "You're entitled to be confused. I get confused sometimes, too."

I swear I heard a whoosh, felt a breeze as the ghost of my razor-sharp father slipped back into the body of this old, muddled man. "Gloria," he said, deadpan. "Call the Alzheimer's clinic. See if they'll give us a father-daughter discount for two."

Gloria and I exchanged guarded smiles. My smart, sarcastic father was back, but for a minute? An hour? We didn't know.

"Let's sit down," Gloria said. My father lowered himself slowly into the grey leather recliner where he spent his upside-down nights and days, reading the paper, calculating the odds for races he'd never see, watching baseball and black-and-white movies on TV. Gloria waved me into the "Hers" recliner that matched my dad's. She sat facing us, perched on a silk damask chair.

For ten years my father had sworn there was nothing for us to talk about. Now, Alzheimer's be damned, he had a speech prepared.

"When it happened," he said without preamble, "I thought you'd come to your senses in a few days." He frowned, grasping at memory. "But then I kept calling you, and you wouldn't talk to me." He turned to Gloria. "Did we have caller ID then?"

"No," she said gently.

My dad turned back to me. "I told Gloria I was more likely to bat for Barry Bonds tomorrow than I was to do that to my daughter."

His expression changed. *Mad Dad.*

"It was unbelievable that I wasn't even speaking to you. I had a plan. I was going to wait until you forgot about me. Then I'd call you and say 'Listen here. This is crazy.' I thought I'd benefit from the element of surprise."

I swallowed hard. "I never forgot about you, Dad."

"I called your mother, too," he went on. "I asked her if there could be any truth to what you were saying."

Oh my God. If he's not sure he didn't do it, how can I be sure? "You called Mom? And that's how you decided that you didn't molest me?"

"You know how it is," my father said. "You hear something often enough, you start to believe it's true."

"Oh, yes," I said. "I do know how that is."

My father's eyes glazed over. "Is it time for lunch?" he asked Gloria.

"We had lunch an hour ago, Stan," Gloria answered. "Right now you're talking to your daughter."

My father shook his head, loosening cobwebs. "Your mother was adamant that nothing happened," he told me. "So finally I said, 'To hell with Meredith. If this doesn't stop, I'm going to take her to court.'"

I shuddered, remembering Gary Ramona testifying against his daughter and her therapists, imagining my dad testifying against me and mine. Then I tried to imagine how I'd feel, what I'd do, if my kids did to me what I'd done to my dad.

"I can understand why you would," I said.

"I'm sure worse things have happened to me," my father said. "But if you asked me to name the second-worst thing," he added, "I couldn't tell you what it was."

Body blow. *That's what I'm here for*, I reminded myself. *To hear his truth. To tell him mine.* "When you accused Stan of abusing you," Gloria interjected, "I started looking at him with totally different eyes. I couldn't sleep at night. I thought, 'Am I lying here next to a child molester?'"

She gazed at me intently. "I almost left my husband," she said.

"I know," I said, remembering our lunch a decade ago, when she'd asked me if she should.

"I thought I knew him pretty well," Gloria continued. "But there were all those stories in the paper at the time, mothers who didn't know their husbands were molesting their daughters."

"I know. I wrote some of those stories."

My father peered at me. "Was it true, what you wrote?" As opposed to what you *said*, he meant.

"I interviewed the daughters. I'm sure they were telling the truth." Unlike me, I meant.

Mad Dad reappeared. "What I really want to know," he said, "is how the hell you could have thought that of me."

A dozen defensive answers rushed to mind. *You turned me against my own mother. You only loved the parts of me that reminded you of you. You said yourself that you had to ask my mother if you'd molested me. How can you be mad at me for wondering?*

He's old, I told myself. He's not well. He did the best he could with his 1950s paradigms and his unexamined life. I had more to work with: my youth, my generation's limitless access to psychological awareness. I should have done better.

"I was wrong to accuse you. I'll regret it for the rest of my life," I answered slowly, carefully, tiptoeing across the tightrope of my complicated truth. "But I don't think it could have happened if we'd had a better relationship when I was a kid."

"There was always a big void in our relationship," my father said dreamily, as if he were in a trance. "In those days, men were supposed to provide for their wives and children. That's what I did. But I wasn't the kind of father your brother is. The kind of father I wish I'd been."

I smiled at him through welling tears. "You weren't such a bad dad," I said.

"I wasn't such a great dad, either," he said. "But I've always loved you."

I gulped around the lump in my throat. "I've never heard you say that before." I realized with a terrible clarity that it was easier to believe that my father had molested me than it was to believe that he loved me.

"You were always something special, right from the start." I watched my father drifting, nostalgia washing over his pale face. "You never walked. You *ran*. The first time we put you in your crib, you'd climbed out by the time we turned around."

My dad peered at me, and I knew what he was seeing. I saw through my kids that way, too: back through time, unchanged in memory.

My belly softened. "I love you, too," I said.

"I feel very much at ease with you, Meredith," my father said. "The closer to now we get, the better it's been."

"Our relationship, you mean?" I asked, wanting to be sure.

My dad nodded, pleased to be understood, and I realized that I'd been doing this all my life: interpreting my father; ascribing meaning to what he'd said and hadn't said, what he'd done and hadn't done. Until this moment, it had never occurred to me that the words and deeds he chose were up to him, but the meanings I chose to extract from his words and his deeds—they were up to me.

"I don't think it ever stopped growing," my dad said.

He blinked at me, his expression pensive. *This is what I've wanted all my life. My father really talking to me. Really listening to me. Really seeing me.*

"Dad," I asked after a decade of wanting to ask, "do you forgive me?"

My father's brow furrowed with concentration. Then he said, with great intensity, "Gloria. What are we having for lunch?"

Grace

January 2010

The doctors had taken my dad's driver's license away months ago. Still, as the BART escalator carried me down to the street, I was surprised to see him in the passenger seat of his baby-blue Camry, parked in our usual Sunday meeting spot.

But there he was, old-school guy, younger wife at the wheel. As soon as he caught a glimpse of me, he leaned out the window, waving wildly. "Over here, Meredith," he yelled.

That loud, nervous voice of his used to drive me nuts—*did* drive me nuts, you might say. But I didn't find my hypervigilant father overbearing and intrusive anymore. I found him goofy and ebullient and sweet.

I slid into the backseat. "Sorry I'm late," I said. "Missed my train."

"No problem," my father said without hesitation. "I rescheduled my afternoon meeting. Mr. Obama was very nice about it. Apparently *his* daughters keep him waiting, too."

"Damn daughters," I said. "Can't live with 'em—"

"Can't live without 'em," my father finished the thought. I hugged him from behind and planted a kiss on his bald, age-spotted head.

Gloria steered the Camry toward the freeway, away from the dim sum restaurant where we often ate our greasy, overstuffed

251

Sunday brunches—with Katrine, with Doug, with Charlie and his girlfriend, with Matthew or Emmy and her daughter when either or both of them were visiting from L.A.

"Your dad says he'll feel more comfortable at home," Gloria explained.

"My dad's *always* felt more comfortable at home," I said.

"No wonder I'm so happy these days," my father said. "That disease I'm supposed to have, whatever it's called—"

"Alzheimer's," Gloria said.

"It gives me the perfect excuse to do what I've always wanted to do."

"Which is . . ." Gloria cued him.

"Absolutely nothing," I said.

"Exactly." My father craned his head around and peered at me. I had a fleeting flashback, a body memory of the years when my father's gaze was everything I craved and everything I feared in this world.

"What's new, daughter?" he asked. "What did you interrupt to come and visit your old man?"

Until a few months ago, I would have found a way to avoid the subject. But nowadays no topic was off-limits between my father and me. Who'da thunk it? There was no one I could be more myself with, now, than my nemesis, my shadow self, my dad.

"I was doing a phone interview for my book," I said.

"Book?" My father frowned, confused or pretending to be.

"My book about my false memory," I reminded him, or played along.

"Oh. *That* book." He paused, composing his comeback. "Maybe I'll pick up a copy. See if it jogs my memory. Ha, ha."

This wrinkle in time—me regaining possession of my mind just as my dad was losing his—was our last chance to know each other as adults, our last chance to turn the powerful charge between us into something sweet and simple and good. I didn't want us to miss a moment of it. So I groaned at his joke and pushed on.

"I was interviewing James Toward, a preschool teacher in Florida," I said. "He went to prison twenty years ago for supposedly molesting a bunch of kids. He's almost eighty now, and he's still there. I'm sure he's innocent."

I wanted my dad to stay with me: ask me questions, agree or disagree. But my body registered that familiar angry, disappointed, empty feeling, his attention slithering away.

"I interviewed one of the kids who testified against him," I said. "She says she was brainwashed by a psychiatrist." I pumped the story up, hoping to lure him back. "She's thirty now. Matthew and Emmy's age."

In the past few years I'd started talking to my father the way I'd talked to my kids when they were very young. Sometimes I felt I'd insulted his considerable intelligence. Sometimes I felt that my language wasn't simple enough to make him understand. Same problem I still had with my grown-up children. Same problem, no doubt, that my dad (and my sons) had with me.

"She's trying to get her teacher out of prison," I said. "She can't forgive herself for sending him there."

My father met my eyes in the rearview mirror. There was nothing demented or forgetful about his gaze. And then he said, with a great sense of import and utterly without rancor, "There but for the grace of God go I."

It was hard to look into my father's eyes, to accept what he was giving me, the gift I'd always wanted: his full attention, no distractions, no jokes. I strained to rise to the occasion. I almost got there, but not quite.

"You don't believe in God, Dad," I teased him. "Remember?"

My father frowned, pondering this. And then looked at me again, his almond-shaped brown eyes—my grandmother's eyes, my eyes, Charlie's eyes—milky with glaucoma and love.

"Better late than never," he said.

"You can say that again," I agreed.

My dad's eyes glittered in the mirror. He shot me that teasing look of his.

"Better late than never," he said again.

acknowledgments

Thank you . . .

For sharing your experiences, research, and reflections: Charlotte Vale Allen, Robert Burton, Katy Butler, George Csicsery, Laura Davis, Carol Diament, Kristin Erickson, Jennifer Freyd, Pamela Freyd, Elizabeth Loftus, Naomi Lowinsky, Lynn Malcom, Jeffrey Masson, Wendy McClure, Debbie Nathan, Mark Pendergrast, Katha Pollitt, Diana Russell, Catherine Stifter, James Toward, and Rosario Toward.

For finding the clips, crunching the stats, and checking the facts: stellar interns Julia Dilday, Elana Fiske, Emma Rae Lierley, and Jess C. Scott.

For reading early drafts and much, much more: Kayne Doumani, Terry Gamble, Jane Juska, Catherine Stifter, Katrine Thomas, and Ayelet Waldman.

For space, time, and solitude: Peter Barnes and Cornelia Durrant, Terry Gamble, Sandra Slater, the Mesa Refuge, the Ragdale Foundation, and the Corporation of Yaddo.

For crucial consultation and steadfast succor: Elisa Tanaka and Toni Burbank. For the author photo minus the goofy grin: Cori Wells Braun and Peter Graham.

To Barb Burg, BB, Best of the Best: publicist, pal, force of nature.

To my agent Linda Loewenthal, collaborator, coach, and friend. No one could do any of it any better than you do. Thank you so much, L.

To the incredible team at Jossey-Bass/Wiley: Erin Beam, Peter Canelias, Carol Hartland, Lesley lura, Michele Jones, Debbie Notkin, Mike Onorato, Jeff Puda, Alan Rinzler, Nana Twumasi, and Jennifer Wenzel.

To my wife, Katrine Andrée Simone Thomas, the brightest star in my night sky; my fluttering heart, my solid ground. *Je t'aime, mon amour.*

And to my brother, my sister-in-law, my sister-out-of-law, my niece, my nephew, my sons, my mother, my stepmother, and my father. I love you, and I thank you, so much, for loving me.

Meredith Maran is an award-winning journalist and the author of several best-selling nonfiction books, including *Dirty, Class Dismissed,* and *What It's Like to Live Now.* Her work appears in anthologies, newspapers, and magazines including *People, Self, Family Circle, More, Mother Jones,* the *San Francisco Chronicle,* and Salon.com. A member of the National Book Critics Circle, she lives in Oakland, California.

book group reading guide

1. How do you define a lie? Are there good lies and bad lies?

2. Have you ever been hurt by a lie? Have you ever hurt others with a lie?

3. Have you ever become convinced of a "truth" that turned out to be false? How did that happen? What were the consequences?

4. Maran quotes a neuroscientist who says, "You're entitled to your own opinion, but you're not entitled to your own facts.?" What's the difference between a belief and a fact?

5. Have you ever done something you deeply regret? Have you tried to redeem yourself? With what results?

6. How would you respond if your child accused you of abuse that you hadn't committed?

7. Were you or was anyone you know sexually abused as a child? How was it handled? What were the repercussions?

8. Do you believe that memories can be repressed and later recovered? Do you think recovered memories should be admissible in court?

9. Maran takes a critical look at therapy in America over the past twenty years. Have you ever been in therapy? Was your experience mostly positive or negative? Did you ever feel that you were being abused or maltreated by

your therapist? If so, did you recognize it at the time, or only in retrospect?

10. Maran seems to conclude that the sex-abuse panic of the 1980s was the product of a combination of factors—within her, and within American society. Which factors seem most significant to you?

11. What do you think of the way Maran handled her marriage, divorce, parenting, false memories?

12. What did you enjoy most about this book? The least?

13. What can we do as a society to prevent another episode like the panic described in My Lie?

14. Did reading My Lie change your thinking about any of these issues?

To share your own responses or those of your reading group, or to invite the author to visit your group, please e-mail Meredith Maran at meredith@meredithmaran.com.